THE REAL GOD

A Response to Anthony Freeman's
God in Us

Richard Harries
Bishop of Oxford

MOWBRAY

Mowbray
A Cassell imprint
Wellington House, 125 Strand, London WC2R 0BB
387 Park Avenue South, New York 10016-8810

First published 1994
Reprinted 1996

British Library Cataloguing-in-Publication Data
A catalogue record is available from the British Library.

ISBN 0-264-67384-0

Printed and bound in Great Britain by
Biddles Ltd, Guildford and King's Lynn

CONTENTS

ACKNOWLEDGEMENTS

I am most grateful to the Revd Professor John Macquarrie and Professor Richard Swinburne and my wife for reading my typescript and for their suggestions.

The publishers thank SCM Press for permission to quote from *God in Us* by Anthony Freeman. The following poems are quoted with kind permission: *Suddenly* by R. S. Thomas, Macmillan London Ltd; *One Foot in Eden* by Edwin Muir, Faber and Faber Ltd.

The cover illustration is Gabriel Loire's East Window in Salisbury Cathedral, reproduced by kind permission of the Dean. Photograph by Pitkin Pictorial. The author photograph is by Frank Blackwell.

Ask, and it will be given you;
Seek, and you will find;
Knock, and it will be opened to you

(Matthew 7.7)

Comfort yourself,
You would not seek me if you had not found me.

(Pascal, *Les Pensées* 7, 553)

God has no better gift to give to those who seek
him than himself. But here is a paradox, that no
one can seek the Lord who has not already found
him. It is thy will oh God, to be found that thou
mayest be sought, to be sought that thou mayest
the more truly be found.

(St Bernard, *On Loving God*, chapter VII)

Costly grace is the Gospel which must be sought
again and again, the gift which must be asked, the
door on which a man must knock.

(Dietrich Bonhoeffer, *The Cost of Discipleship*)

O Lord, teach me to seek thee, and reveal thyself
to me when I seek thee. For I cannot seek thee
unless thou teach me, nor find thee except thou
reveal thyself. Let me seek thee in longing, let
me long for thee in seeking; let me find thee in
love, and love thee in finding.

(St Ambrose)

INTRODUCTION

In his book *God in Us*,[1] Anthony Freeman maintains that the word 'God' refers only to human values and ideals. If the world was destroyed, there would be no God; if for some reason human language ceased to exist so would God. There is nothing outside us, to which God language refers. Indeed there is nothing outside our language.

Freeman is not alone in this view. He has put in popular and combative form the basic outlook of the 'Sea of Faith' group associated with Don Cupitt of Cambridge. This in turn draws its impetus from currents of thought derived from post-modernism and deconstructionism.

The present debate about God is significantly different from previous ones. The question of whether or not God 'exists' has always been around. In the 1960s and 1970s under the influence of first logical positivism and then linguistic philosophy, the debate focused on the nature of religious language. For example, does a sentence like 'God loves the world' merely express the speaker's personal preference or commitment or does it assert something definite that might be open to verification or falsification?

At the same time as that debate was continuing (and still is) a popular debate was taking place about whether we should think of God as 'the ground of our being' or as 'the beyond in our midst'. Associated with thinkers like Paul Tillich and Dietrich Bonhoeffer and made accessible through the work of John Robinson in *Honest to God*, it was a discussion that went off in a number of directions. One extreme form was the so-called 'Death of God' school. The motivation behind this debate was, in my view, primarily pastoral, psychological and political rather than strictly philosophical. The underlying pastoral issues present then are still with us and have surfaced again in the current debate.

The new twist in the present discussion is the notion that questions of meaning and truth are no longer capable of being answered in an objective manner. People are understandably puzzled by words like post-modernism and deconstructionism. After all do we not still live in a very modern world? How can it be called post-modernism? Modernism refers primarily to the movement in the arts just before and after the Second World War, in music, poetry, painting and writing, when traditional forms were challenged and exciting new forms of artistic expression emerged. But at this time and indeed until shortly after the Second World War, people still had some confidence that we could get at the real meaning of a literary text or at what really happened in some historical period. Post-modernism on the other hand refers to a world in which we are all acutely conscious of cultural differences, the way that people in different historical periods see things so variously, the endlessly shifting interpretations of everything and the fact that we are all bedded down as particular individuals, in a particular period of history, shaped by the very language we use to think about anything. The result, it is alleged, is that we can never get to the real meaning or truth of anything. There are some important insights in this post-modernist view of the universe. But, as I shall argue, questions of meaning and truth still remain very much on the agenda.

In contrast to Freeman's view that all we have of God is our language of God, with no remainder, I believe that God is real.

The word 'real' is slippery and people have made it mean many things. Materialists, for example, assume that only what we can touch and feel and weigh is real. Adherents of eastern philosophy on the other hand assume that this world is a kind of illusion and they therefore pray 'Lead us from the unreal to the real'. In saying that God is real, I mean three things.

First, God exists outside my mind, as the circumference of a circle exists outside its centre. My mind, and every mind, is the centre of a sphere whose radius is infinite. From time to time there arise people who think that everything that exists is simply a product of their imagination, a dream; a view technically known as solipsism. If I say that you are part of my dream and you reply 'But I am not, here I am speaking to you', a solipsist can always reply that your response is also part of my mind's projection or dream. Solipsism is notably difficult to refute philosophically, except by Dr Johnson's common-sense recourse of stubbing his foot against a stone. Nevertheless it is a fundamental assumption for most of us that there is indeed a world outside our minds, that other people exist and that we can discern aspects of this world which can be judged more or less true or more or less false. In a similar way a realist view of God asserts that there is a spiritual milieu, in which we live and move and have our being, but which is not confined to or limited by the language which we use about it.

Second, this spiritual milieu is closely connected to our struggle for integrity, and therefore is linked with fundamental moral values. Plato believed that in seeking the *kalon*, the good and the beautiful, we were seeking something that really existed, absolutely, independently of its manifestation in good people or beautiful objects. Few people today would be able to subscribe to that kind of view; nevertheless many people (and I would argue all people at one time or another in their lives) are haunted by the importance of the moral quest. Novelists, who get inside people's skins, are able to convey this sense better than any philosophers. In the novels of Dostoyevsky or William Golding, we get the sense that something ultimate is at stake, in even the most outwardly insignificant or apparently useless life. So it is not just a question of moral philosophy, about whether words like right and wrong or good and bad refer to anything other than our own preferences, but of the sense, shared by so many, that in striving to live with dignity and courage and an element of selflessness something ultimate is at stake, that life is more than a calculus of pleasure and pain. Albert Camus said that the one fundamental question of human existence was that of suicide. Sadly, something like 5,000 people a year in Great Britain commit suicide. Yet despite what are sometimes the most appalling circumstances most people somehow struggle on. I believe that this is more than a biological will to life. It reflects an inchoate conviction that we live in a moral universe whose values are not ones that we simply happen to choose but which impinge upon us.

Third, we live in a sacramental world, that is, the outward and visible manifests that which is inward and spiritual. 'The world is charged with the grandeur of God', as Hopkins puts it.

Oscar Wilde once said that there ought to be a religion for people like him who were out-and-out sensualists, that is people who rejoice in the physical and material and who find it virtually impossible to move beyond this to envisage what is invisible. Most of us today would have a great deal of sympathy with this view of Oscar Wilde. The Christian approach, however, is not one of escape from this world to another world altogether. It is rather a question of rejoicing in this world and seeing it as a sign or sacrament of a larger whole. As Simone Weil once put it:

> The beauty of the world is Christ's tender smile for us coming through matter. He is really present in the universal beauty. The love of his beauty precedes from God dwelling in our souls and goes out to God present in the universe. It is also like a sacrament.[2]

Theologians and mystics have always been acutely conscious of how limited our language is in talking about God. They have always stressed the crucial importance of the *via negativa*, or the apophatic way, the fact that everything we say about God is as untrue as it is true and therefore, that we need to qualify and unmake images as soon as we have suggested them.

This is the theme of T.S. Eliot's *Four Quartets* as of the poetry of R.S. Thomas in our own time. But the God before whose mystery we must properly be silent is nevertheless real. This is a God to whom I can relate, to whom I can pray, to whom I can respond. This is a God who wills to make himself known in response to our seeking; a God whose glory has shone in the humility of Christ and who through the Holy Spirit illuminates our minds now.

Through all hesitations, doubts and protests something can be said about the real God, the one who is not simply a human construct, but one who wills to touch our hearts and change our lives. More than any other writer of our time, R.S. Thomas has explored the absence and silence of God. Yet he is also capable of writing:

> Suddenly after long silence
> he has become voluble.

He addresses me from a myriad
directions with the fluency
of water, the articulateness
of green leaves; and in the genes,
too, the components
of my existence. The rock,
so long speechless, is the library
of his poetry. He sings to me
in the chain-saw, writes
with the surgeon's hand
on the skin's parchment messages
of healing. The weather
is his mind's turbine
driving the earth's bulk round
and around on its remedial
journey. I have no need
to despair; as at
some second Pentecost
of a Gentile, I listen to the things
round me: weeds, stones, instruments,
the machine itself, all
speaking to me in the vernacular
of the purposes of One who is.[3]

Chapter 1

GETTING RID OF
THE OPPRESSOR

C.S. Lewis once complained that it had become customary for theologians to let themselves off a clear answer. This accusation cannot be made against Anthony Freeman. His book is not only readable, it makes it quite clear where he stands. His 'Case for Christian humanism' offers an unmistakable challenge to traditional believers. It is, to use a word of the author, 'bracing'. Like the breezes of Skegness this could be good for us. Yet it might also be that everything has been blown off the beach into the sea.

I believe that the questions raised by Mr Freeman are important and they need to be faced. Although his views may not be held by many, the underlying feelings and questions that give rise to them are widely shared. It is the purpose of my own response to examine these feelings and face those questions; and to give answers without equivocation. The answers will be very different from those of Mr Freeman but I would stress that the pastoral context in which these issues arise is shared by both of us and needs to be taken with the utmost seriousness. I am not in the business of propaganda or point-scoring. What is at stake is nothing less than the truth.

Mr Freeman begins his book with two prayers from the 1662 *Book of Common Prayer*. The first, for the Queen, stresses the kingship of God: 'whose Kingdom is everlasting, and power infinite'. The second is a prayer for fair weather. He then goes on to discuss two assassination attempts, one in which the Pope was badly injured but survived and the other in which President Kennedy was killed. No one, he argues, believes in an intervening God today, for, in relation to the Pope:

Either God was monumentally incompetent in not upsetting

the aim enough to miss the Pope altogether; or else God deliberately allowed the Pope to be injured – but not fatally. Neither suggestion was made. Because no one really believes in that kind of intervention any more.

In relation to President John Kennedy:

He was the leader of the world's most powerful nation. It was a time of great international tension. If God had an interventionist day to day concern with world affairs it could hardly have been a matter of indifference to him. Yet no one printed headlines such as: *God's judgement on Kennedy administration* or *Marksman's miraculous aim.* The absence of any miraculous intervention to save John Kennedy went quite unremarked.

After outlining three possible approaches to belief, the conservative, the liberal and the radical, Freeman writes that when he moved from being a liberal to a radical, he felt a great sense of relief. The liberal goes on struggling with the old dilemmas of how God relates to the world and how a God of love can allow such incidents. But a radical is freed from all that:

Radicals say that we do not need to bring in the supernatural at all. It belongs to that long-gone world of the past. It may have a place in fairy tales and horror films but it has no place in our understanding of the real world. All aspects of our life – physical, mental, aesthetic, moral, spiritual – all are human in origin and content. To invoke the supernatural is unnecessary, because they can explain all aspects of our life without it.

The approach in this book cannot, I think, be neatly labelled conservative, liberal or radical and such stereotypes are usually unhelpful. My concern is simply to examine the arguments, as carefully and truthfully as possible. To begin with we need to distinguish three aspects of the challenge which is put forward so forcefully.

First, there is the question of religious imagery. I do not find it particularly helpful to think of the kingship of God. Certainly,

such a metaphor is nowhere near the heart of my faith. Although
we live in a monarchy, which I support, it does not have the
same reality as it did for the compilers of the Prayer Books in
1549, 1552 and 1662. I look to other pictures and metaphors to
draw my heart to God, ones that have moral and spiritual appeal
today. There is no shortage of them in the Bible, in the tradition
of Christian literature and in modern writing. In the latter
category there is T.S. Eliot's image of God as 'the wounded
surgeon'.[4] It is a similar image which W.H. Vanstone developed
so memorably in his book *Love's Endeavour, Love's Expense.*[5]
There he tells the story of an early operation on the brain. The
surgeon was in the operating theatre all day. At the end, he was
so utterly drained he had to be led out by the hand. With total
attention he had given himself completely to the task. Vanstone
suggests that God's creation of the world is like this. Creation is
not something he undertook lightly. He gives himself totally to
it, he pours himself into his work.

It would also be possible to take any of Janet Morley's
prayers,[6] for example that for the ninth Sunday before Easter:

> Vulnerable God,
> You challenge the powers that rule this world
> Through the needy, the compassionate,
> And those who are filled with longing.
> Make us hunger and thirst to see right prevail,
> And single-minded in seeking peace;
> That we may see your face
> And be satisfied in you,
> Through Jesus Christ, Amen.

Or the prayer for Julian of Norwich's day (8 May) which takes
up some of her imagery:

> Christ our true Mother,
> You have carried us within you,
> Laboured with us,
> And brought us forth to bliss.
> Enclose us in your care,
> That in stumbling we may not fall,
> Nor be overcome by evil,

But know that all shall be well, Amen.

Many other metaphors, modern or ancient, could have been chosen but they will have similar characteristics. They put before us a God who is vulnerable, who suffers with us and for us, a God who works his purpose in the world not by arbitrary power but by patient invitation; a God whose qualities are as feminine as they are masculine.

This does not mean that images of God's kingship need to be totally discarded. On the contrary they have their proper place. When taking prayers in the House of Lords I am glad of sentiments that refer to God as 'King of Kings and Lord of Lords'. For they remind all of us that human power is held on trust from God and is accountable to him. But such prayers do not, for most of us, take us to the heart of our faith in God. Fortunately for that, there are a good number of metaphors with a profound moral and spiritual appeal and we are entirely at liberty to look for them and use them.

Second, we have to distinguish questions about God's reality from questions about how God relates to the world. The examples that Anthony Freeman gives concern the latter, not the former. They make the point that, so it seems, God does not directly 'intervene' in the world to stop assassination attempts, even when the person is of the utmost religious importance (the Pope) or of political importance at a time of international tension (President Kennedy). However, this in no way answers the question whether or not God is real. For God could still be very much there, holding all things in existence, enfolding all things with his love and filling all things with his spirit but may nevertheless deliberately not 'intervene', for very good reasons.

An 18-year-old borrows the family car and has a bad accident. Everyone is distressed and the parents question whether they should have given him permission to take the car out. Yet, sooner or later, if we are to grow up at all, we have to do things on our own including, for most people today in Britain, drive a car. The parents are certainly there in the background and they love their son dearly: but it is an essential expression of that love that they leave him free, at the appropriate time, to run his own life and make his own mistakes.[7]

I am not of course suggesting that this analogy by itself shows that God is real – simply that the question of God's reality and the question of how he relates to his world can and should be kept distinct. The fact that he does not, apparently, 'intervene' in a direct and obvious way should not be taken as evidence that he is not truly there. The whole question of how we might think of God's relationship to the world, particularly a world in which there is so much evil and suffering, will be considered later.

Third, there is a question about the sense of liberation that Freeman felt when he gave up the traditional concept of a transcendent God. 'It was not a conversion from unbelief to faith, but from a Christianity which had become oppressive to one which brought a glorious sense of freedom and joy.'

There is no doubt that for some people the faith has been felt to be oppressive and unbelief has come as a relief. 'Tears, tears, tears of joy', wrote Jean-Paul Sartre, 'There is no God.' This is usually because the religion in which the person has been brought up has been put across as or understood to be anti-life, or anti-this-world, or anti-art in its widest sense. In James Joyce's novel *A Portrait of the Artist as a Young Man*, Stephen Dedalus was seriously debating in his mind whether he should become a priest when one day, as he walked on the beach, life, as he put it, took hold of him. He described his mood in these words:

> His throat ached with a desire to cry aloud, the cry of a hawk or eagle on high, to cry piercingly of his deliverance to the winds. This was the call of life to his soul not the dull gross voice of the world of duties and despair, not the inhuman voice that had called him to the pale service of the altar ... His soul had arisen from the grave of boyhood, spurning her grave clothes ... The clouds were drifting above him silently and silently the sea tangle was drifting below him and the grey warm air was still and a new wild life was singing in his veins.[8]

He decides to leave Ireland altogether and the night before he goes he wrote in his diary: 'Welcome, O life! I go to encounter for the millionth time the reality of experience.'[9]

This experience could be paralleled many times, particularly by those who have had a strict religious upbringing, whether

Catholic or Protestant.

Freud explained the psychological roots of this sense of oppression with the help of his concept of the super-ego. There is no doubt that some people have a harsh super-ego and that this can become combined with a picture of God who is oppressive, making us feel small, dirty or guilty. Disbelief in this God does indeed come as a great relief. The crucial question though is whether any and every concept of a transcendent God must of its nature be oppressive. Some forms of atheistic protest, Nietzsche's for example, would certainly view every concept of God as inimical to human autonomy. Yet this is like saying that every parent or every friend must be oppressive. It is certainly true that all parents, by their very existence and role, are an 'other' with whom the growing child must reckon. But so is a friend. The fact is that all realities, just because they are truly there and are not simply a fantasy or a projection of what we would like, confront us with their own claims. These claims may be those of a friend, or a child or a parent, or God. For the real God is really God, the one who by definition makes a total difference to my life, one whom I cannot know simply as an object in the world of objects, but whom I can only come to believe in as the God of my life as well as of the universe. It means acknowledging reality: that I am finite, a creature, dependent upon the ground of being as I am upon the ground I walk on or the air I breathe. Some may find this oppressive. But the pressure of reality, whether of God or a friend, is to be sharply distinguished from an inner tyrant who might have been introjected as the result of an unsatisfactory upbringing or a bad experience of religion. H.A. Williams described his deliverance from such a God – it led him in and through a breakdown. He also came to believe in a God in us. But a God who is in us because he is first other than us. This God, being real, will never be simply the product of our wishful thinking. Inevitably we all make God partly in our image; the God in whom we believe will always be to some extent a God we most want or a God we most fear. But faith, especially as expressed in prayer, will for a believer also involve struggle and wrestling with that which is other than us. As Charles Wesley's great hymn puts it:

Come, O thou traveller unknown,

Whom still I hold, but cannot see;
My company before is gone,
And I am left alone with thee;
With thee all night I mean to stay
And wrestle till the break of day.

What I have suggested so far is, first, that we can give ourselves permission to put aside pictures of God we find unhelpful, which 'do not speak to our condition' and we can instead focus on and meditate upon those which move us and evoke in us a desire for God. We are certainly not tied to any seventeenth century concept of kingship.

Second, the question of whether God is real needs to be separated from the question of how he relates to us. The fact that God does not 'intervene' in any obvious way is no indication that he is not there. Moment by moment he holds us and all things in being and enables every constituent part of the universe, in the microcosm and the macrocosm, to go on being itself. Whether more than this can be said will be explored later.

Third, some forms of faith have certainly been experienced as oppressive, psychologically as well as politically. To abandon this God can indeed be a great relief. But this still leaves open the possibility of a true God, one who helps us to believe in ourselves and our worth and gives us confidence in the creative springs within us. Yet even that God, just because he is real, will like all reality surprise us and touch us in unexpected ways.

Chapter 2

HOW DO WE BELIEVE?

People have often asserted that there are two ways in which we can know God and something about him. First, by reflecting on the sheer existence of the world we can come to the conclusion that there is a Creator. Second, God has chosen to disclose something of his mind and purpose to us, for example that we can relate to him like children to a trustworthy father.

Freeman discusses both these approaches and concludes that neither the first (natural theology) nor the second (revealed theology) gives us any knowledge of God at all.

The first approach focuses on the traditional 'proofs' for the existence of God, including the argument from causality and the argument from design. I believe I am even more sceptical about such proofs than Freeman. It is simply not possible on grounds of logic alone to convince the unbeliever. But it is important to see both why they do not work and why, despite this, they have a continuing appeal.

The argument from causality moves from the fact that there is nothing in this world which happens without a cause, to the conclusion the universe itself must have one. To the child's question that if this is God, then who made God, the only answer can be that God is by definition the uncaused cause, the origin of all that is but himself self-sufficient and eternal.

Over the years a number of refutations of this argument have been put forward but I still think that the most valid is that of Immanuel Kant. He pointed out that although everything that happens within human experience does indeed have a cause, we do not know whether the argument from effects to causes can apply to the universe as a whole. We do not know if this kind of logical reasoning holds good. The traditional argument to a first cause worked on the assumption that the same kind of reasoning applies to the universe as a whole as is used within it. But this is an assumption that has as it were been smuggled in. All we can

do is say that God considered as the uncaused cause of the
universe is a 'regulative idea'. This idea certainly caps a process
of reasoning in a very neat way and it helps make sense of why
the universe is here at all. But all this presupposes that the chain
of cause and effect is applicable to existence as such in the same
way as it is to particular existences – and it is just this which is
in question. The so-called proof therefore must always leave the
matter open. For those who would like to see the world as the
product of a rational intelligence, it would be nice. But on the
basis of logic alone, we do not know whether this is so.

The argument from design starts from our sense of wonder
before the intricacy and marvel of the world and suggests that as
for example a computer needs a human designer, so must the
world have a divine designer. Why this argument does not work
is even easier to see. In order to say whether anything is
designed or not we have to have a standard of comparison: and
by definition there is only one universe. In my garden is an
asparagus bed. In another part of the garden recently I
discovered a single asparagus growing in a flower bed. I know
that the asparagus bed, has been designed because it has all the
marks that I have seen in other designed asparagus beds: it is
laid out symmetrically, the soil has been manured, boards hold
the soil up and so on. Because the single asparagus in the flower
bed does not have these marks I assume that its presence is the
result of birds or animals carrying a seed or baby stalk.

When it comes to the universe, I do not have a category of
designed universes to compare with another category that have
somehow sprung up of themselves. There is only one universe.
(There may very well be many worlds in addition to this one but
by definition the God with whom we are concerned is the
Creator of all possible worlds, i.e. the universe.) So we are
simply not in a position, on the basis of logic, to say whether the
universe is designed or not. The matter is open. This has
important implications for the work of people like Richard
Dawkins, who show through a process of natural selection and
random mutation how the most complex and beautiful forms can
evolve from simple ones over a long period of time. I have no
reason to doubt that what Dawkins is saying from a scientific
point of view is right. But this does not prove that there is no
divine designer. For there could be a designer who put the whole

process of evolution in place, with its thrust to produce complexity out of simplicity until the arrival of us human beings on the scene. The argument always leaves the matter open. Darwin himself was a devout believer in the early part of his life and gradually became more agnostic. But this was not because of the process of evolution as such but its apparently cruel character. Freeman seems to feel the same way: 'Nor can I accept any longer ... that a good and skilful God would have designed so much waste and violence into nature, "red in tooth and claw".' I very much sympathize with this point. But it is a separate issue that needs to be dealt with later. An understanding of evolution as such simply enlarges our understanding of God and how he works. As Frederick Temple put it in the nineteenth century, in a fine phrase, 'God makes the world make itself.' His hand is always hidden. Whether there really is a hidden hand or no hand at all cannot be settled either by the argument from design or a scientific description of how the process works.[10]

There are other reasons why such arguments do not do what they set out to do, reasons that come from the side of faith. A person could come to the end of a logical train of argument with the conclusion that God must, logically, exist: and it could leave him stone cold. This points to the fact that knowledge of God is more like knowing a person than it is knowing that there is a deck chair in the garden. God is not of course a 'person' as we are persons and this raises the whole question of religious language and how it refers to God at all, which will be considered later. But all religions of the world, except for certain forms of Buddhism, claim that the concept of relationship is appropriate to ultimate reality.

In order to know another person two conditions must be fulfilled. First, the partners to the relationship must be willing to share something of themselves and, second, they must be willing to enter into a relationship which involves a degree of intimacy.

When it comes to knowing God, there is a further condition. I must be willing to enter into a relationship with a reality who by definition makes a total difference to the way I view life and myself. God is not an object in the world of objects, like a pen that can be looked at and handled from every angle, weighed and measured and drawn. That is why theologians are wary of using the word 'exist' about God at all. For God does not exist as

stones and houses exist, as a thing in the world of things. Rather
God is the source of all that exists, the ground of being. When
we meet a friend we can make a distinction between knowing
that the friend actually exists and knowing him or her as a
person. We cannot make such a neat distinction in relation to
God. For we cannot know that God exists, in a neutral way, as
though we could stand over him to look and describe. We can
only know God as God; that is, as I know myself as a creature in
relation to a creator.

It is therefore because of these considerations, as well as the
purely logical ones, that the so-called 'proofs' for the existence
of God cannot achieve their purpose.

I believe that the traditional distinction between natural
theology, on the basis of which we know that God exists, and
revealed theology, through which we know something about
him, is not helpful. Any knowledge we may have of God is
dependent both upon his willingness to disclose something of his
purpose to us and our willingness to respond to this. So I prefer
to speak of natural religion. What I mean is this.

It is natural for a child to believe that there is a creator of the
world. A child makes instinctive use of the argument from
causality. If the child has been brought up in a family imbued
with trust and kindness, it is again entirely natural for that child
to think that the creator is also kind and trustworthy.
Furthermore, it is not only natural for children to make this
movement of the heart, as so many of them do, it is natural in the
sense that trust comes before mistrust. It is a pre-condition of
any kind of human relationship that we trust most people most of
the time to mean more or less what they say. A settled attitude of
total distrust or cynicism would preclude the possibility of any
kind of relationship at all. Of course we come to mistrust
particular people, we are hurt and let down and we quite
properly develop habits of discrimination and criticism. But,
nevertheless, trust is prior, in the sense that it is a presupposition
or precondition of the possibility of any kind of relationship at
all.

The same holds good in relation to the possibility that there
might be a wise and loving power behind this strange, painful
universe of ours. We may come to disbelieve. The terrible
suffering and anguish in human life, the apparent futility and

pointlessness of so many lives, may in the end drain away any
residue of faith. With absolute sincerity we may simply find it
impossible to believe. But a settled attitude of scepticism from
the outset would preclude any possibility of belief, even if there
is a God. So trust is also prior here, in the sense of an openness
to the possibility of there being a wise and loving power. In this
sense faith, a sincere openness to the possibility of God, is
natural. And that is why those parents who are themselves
agnostic but who choose to give their children a religious
upbringing are right, despite the apparent contradiction of their
position. For openness to the possibility of a wise and loving
power behind life keeps both the option of belief and unbelief
open. A settled scepticism from the outset precludes the
possibility of belief.

There is also another rather more obvious sense in which
religion is natural. All civilizations and cultures that the world
has so far known have been built upon a religious vision and
understanding of life. People have had to think themselves out of
the predominant belief of their culture and this has required a
fair amount of independence of mind.

I am not by these considerations wanting to argue that religion
is therefore true. It could be natural, in the ways I have
described, and still be false. The case against the possibility of a
good God at the origin of Creation is a formidable one. But it is
important that the case against God be located in the proper
place, and that has to do with the character of the universe.

I stress the importance of natural religion, as opposed to
natural theology, because what I have described is, I think, the
way in fact most people believe or come to believe. They are not
on the whole argued into a belief by a process of logical
reasoning. They are either brought up in a home, where it is part
of the way of life, or they come across people who have
something that attracts them and, gradually or suddenly, the
claims of religion take hold. It is this actual, living experience of
a religion which is so crucial. Nevertheless, in appealing to
religion as natural, I want to make two points quite clear.

First, I am not appealing to extraordinary or exotic manifest-
ations of religious experience, visions, voices or miracles. I refer
simply to the fact that ordinary Christian believers claim to have
a relationship with God, to whom they pray. In the decisions of

life they seek the guidance of the Holy Spirit. In the stresses and strains they seek the help of God's grace. They try to follow Christ by responding to the opportunities which each day provide for service of one kind or another. Furthermore, they see themselves as very much part of a long and vital tradition. Their personal faith might burn low from time to time but they are conscious of being upheld by the writings and examples of those whose faith seems stronger or more convinced than theirs.

Second, there is no way in which this claimed experience of God can be made the basis of an argument for his reality which will convince the non-believer. For if someone says that God is a reality in their life, it is always open to someone else to give a psychological or social explanation of this and the argument can never be settled one way or the other. It is always possible to give a psychological explanation of both belief and disbelief. I have read convincing accounts of the psychological process whereby Freud became an atheist. But this does not of itself make his views invalid. Those views, like the claims of religion, have to be argued for and against in other terms. Simply to point to the psychological process which leads to belief or disbelief does not prove or disprove the truth of this belief.

If the account of belief that I have set out does in fact accord with what happens, then this sheds some light on the so-called proofs for the existence of God, proofs which as I suggested always leave the matter open. A Christian believer (and for that matter a Jew, a Muslim or any other monotheist) looking at the argument from causality will always tend to have some sympathy with it and want to go along with it, because he or she already believes that there is a Creator. Because their heart already moves in gratitude from Creation to Creator, it is natural for their mind to move in that direction as well. Cardinal Newman once wrote that: 'The whole man moves, paper logic is but the record of it.' I believe this is too extreme and that logic can act as the helmsman of the ship, not simply a log book of where we have been. Nevertheless, Newman's remark does bring out the important truth, that our great shifts of belief or disbelief are never purely intellectual, they involve the whole person. So, because we know God in our own life, we will naturally believe him to be present in the life of the world of which we are a part. Scientists can describe the visible process whereby the universe came into being, the 'big bang'. Neither they, nor anyone else, can describe in scientific terms the divine power which brings about that process *ex nihilo*. But there is one point where we do experience God's creative action. As Austin Farrer has written:

There is only one point at which we can possibly touch the nerve of God's creative action, or experience creation taking place: and that is in our own life. The believer draws his active Christian existence out of the wellspring of divine creation, he prays prayers which become the very act of God's will in his will. Because we have God under the root of our being we cannot help but acknowledge him at the root of all the world's being.[11]

A similar movement of the heart and mind takes place in relation to the process of evolution. Any divine pressure there might be leading matter to evolve into life, then life to evolve into self-conscious life, is totally hidden. But the believer does know something of that pressure in his or her own life. We know the interaction of our will with the divine will. We also know that in order to create any one of us God had to create a universe. The whole universe comes to a focus in us. So we in faith believe that the same divine will has been active at every point in the evolutionary process. It will be that a believer, struck again by the complexity, wonder and beauty of the world, will find that his or her mind moves to acknowledge the wonder of the Creator and the heart to praise. The argument from design, as it, were traces out the journey that the heart of the believer makes and the mind finds it natural to make that journey because it already believes.

I have tried to show in this chapter that for believers, it is their own sense of the reality of God, however weak and flickering, that is of crucial importance, especially when they are aware that they are part of a great community of faith. It is absurd to pretend that we believe by a process of logical argument. Most of us do not. A person who is already predisposed to believe in God, who is searching and willing to believe, may very often find the arguments a help. But they can never act as proof for the total sceptic. They indicate a journey of the mind that the heart is already in the process of making.

So what about the person who stands outside the charmed circle of belief? How on earth can they get inside? The fact that some people believe and others do not is a mystery, to which there is no definite answer. It is clearly not a matter of intellect alone. Most of the distinguished minds in human history have been believers, some have not. I suspect that most of those who disbelieve do so because they have had a bad experience of religion. Some do so because their understanding of religion is full of misconceptions. Some may be unwilling to make the necessary changes in lifestyle which the Christian faith asks of us. Others see no way of reconciling the tragic quality of so much existence with the claim that there is a loving Creator. There is a variety of reasons, all of which have to be looked at separately. My claim in this chapter is that religious faith is natural to us as human beings. It is natural for the heart of a child to move to the thought of a good Creator. And it is right that this should be so, whether or not there is a good Creator, because openness to this possibility is the only way in which genuine belief can come or develop. Disbelief needs to be taken with the utmost seriousness, but it is secondary. People cannot be argued into belief. All we can do is try to set out the faith as clearly as possible and dispel some of the many misunderstandings and misconceptions which so distort the discussion. When the faith has been set forth and the misunderstandings patiently cleared up the person may find that they believe – or they may not. In any case, faith cannot be manufactured. It comes as a response to what is set forth. What is set forth takes hold of the hearer – or it does not. This seems to imply that whether one believes or not is entirely arbitrary and irrational. This is not the case. There are rational considerations that can and must be adduced, which will be later discussed in chapter nine.

Chapter 3

THE GOD WHO MAKES HIMSELF KNOWN

As already mentioned there are, traditionally, two ways to the knowledge of God: reflection on the world (natural theology) and God's self-disclosure (revealed theology). In the last chapter I indicated I did not accept this hard and fast distinction, preferring the concept of natural religion, concluding that all our knowledge of God (including his existence) is dependent on his willingness to make himself known and our willingness to know. But, in any case, the God in whom I believe is one who wants to make his character and purpose known to us. Freeman says that claimed revelations of God get us nowhere. We can learn nothing at all about God from them. He seems to have three reasons for this scepticism.

First, every book of the Bible has a historical context and a human author or authors. In many cases we can discover when a book was written, by whom, with what purpose and under what social and political conditions. If there is a God behind these writings, or some part of them, we just do not know because they always come to us through particular human beings in a particular historical context. The same is true of all appeals to religious experience. People claim to know Christ or experience the presence of God in some way but 'divine revelation (if it does exist) is always human at the point of delivery'.

Second, what claims to be revealed varies greatly from age to age. We can see how Christian doctrines, for example, change and develop in response to the circumstances and prevailing philosophy of the age in which they are stated.

Third, because each age makes its own interpretation and these inevitably vary greatly, our own generation will both inevitably and quite properly state the faith in our terms. And because past understandings are so obviously the product of

specific and historical human factors, Freeman makes this his
own cardinal principle. He will regard all God talk as being
simply the expression of human values and ideals.

Now, it is quite possible to acknowledge a significant element
of truth in the first two points, without drawing the conclusions
in his third one. I fully accept that all claimed relevation,
whether in the Bible or elsewhere, is 'human at the point of
delivery' and that each age makes its own interpretation. But it
does not follow that all we have is nothing but the product of
human factors or that we can today interpret the faith in a way
that totally evacuates the word God of its traditional meaning. I
do not draw his conclusion for a number of reasons.

I am as often struck by our continuity with the past as I am by
the discontinuity. It is a great gain for modern scholarship,
particularly biblical scholarship, that we now recognize that in
some respects past periods of history are very different from our
own. Many of the New Testament writings for example are
steeped in a sense that the consummation of history, the
Kingdom of God, is to come very soon, a view that is not shared
by our culture as a whole.

Recognizing such differences is important. But when, for
example, I read Pliny's account of the destruction of Pompeii by
the eruption of Vesuvius and the behaviour of his uncle at the
time, I am conscious of a person I can recognize, someone with
feelings and an approach to life which I might encounter in our
own society. Or when I read a letter of Gregory of Nyssa about
how wonderful it is to get away into a quiet valley to enjoy
nature, think and pray, I know the feeling. The continuities of
history are as striking as the discontinuities. Further, it is on the
basis of these continuities that we are able to enter into the past
to understand past societies and peoples. If it was all totally
alien, with no point of contact, we could not engage with it. We
might be able to write an external description of buildings or an
ancient document but we would not be able to enter imaginatively into that other world. With Christian writers, I feel that
world is so often very close to my own. Western scholarship has
been so concerned with historical contexts that it has sometimes
lost the sense of a living tradition which is still present in
Orthodoxy. As Donald Allchin has written, about a visit to a
monastery:

One day the Abbot took me to see the monastery library. It was not a very large collection of books. There were a lot of elderly, well-used volumes of the Fathers. 'Here', said the Abbot, 'is a book which you give to beginners.' 'This is a work which is useful for someone who is depressed.' 'Here is a book which will give very clear instructions about the Jesus Prayer.' Any Westerner showing you round this collection of books, even some-one to whom they were of practical use, would have said: 'Here is an interesting sixth century text.' 'This writer shows influences from the Syrian tradition,' 'Here is a work important in the later development of Hesychasm.' We look at books chronologically and classify them in terms of influences and development. To the Abbot they all had a simultaneous existence and composed a simultaneous order. They were all books which were useful for life in the Spirit. Their authors were fathers and teachers who had become friends, to whom one spoke in church and at other times; it was of little importance whether they had lived six hundred, twelve hundred or fifty years ago. He showed me the library rather in the way in which an expert gardener might show you his collection of books on gardening, or a cook a collection of cookery books. These help you on your way. They are not an end in themselves.[12]

Although Christian beliefs do indeed develop in relation to the circumstances and philosophy of a particular time and they are often expressed differently in different ages or cultures, it is still possible to be strongly aware of a Christian identity. We might take the analogy of a school. It was founded in the sixteenth century for twelve clever but poor boys from the town. In the nineteenth century it became a large boys' grammar school. In the twentieth century it went .co-educational and comprehensive. It is still however in a profound sense the school that was founded, even though it may be on a totally different site and with a different curriculum: and the annual Founder's Day service acknowledges this continuity of identity. Identity can remain despite manifold changes. Equally, identity can clearly be lost. If as a result of falling rolls in the area that school decided to close but let its buildings be used as an arts centre, we would probably judge that there had been a change of identity. But the Christian Church has retained its identity over many centuries and in many different cultures. For example, few changes are as stark as the way the faith has been expressed in the visual arts. The art of the catacombs of Rome in the third century is very different from the art of Ravenna in the sixth, which in turn is very different from, say, the art of Botticelli in the late fifteenth century or that of Liverpool's Roman Catholic Cathedral in our own time. The art of the catacombs is that of a small, mostly hidden and sometimes persecuted sect. That of Ravenna is that of a glittering Christian civilization, presided over by the Emperor. The art of Botticelli draws on the technical advances of the Italian Renaissance as well as some of the neo-Platonism that was around at the time, whilst the Cathedral not only reflects a twentieth-century understanding of the Liturgy in its design; it seeks to state the faith in a cultural climate which values abstract art. Yet it only takes a minimum of reflection and imagination for a Christian to appreciate the images of redemption in the catacombs, the concept of the Eucharist in the apse mosaic of San Vitale in Ravenna, the joy of Botticelli's mystic Nativity or the sense of light and glory of Ceri Richards' Sacrament Chapel in Liverpool Cathedral. Quite properly each age will have its own emphasis, it will down-play some aspects of the tradition and draw out others. It will both reflect and seek to relate to the culture of the time. But there is a tradition with a definite identity, to which we feel we can belong.

It is also a tradition that has its own built-in criteria for distinguishing what belongs and what does not. Manichaeism was rejected, because the material world is good not evil. Gnosticism was rejected by the Christian Church because Christianity is not a secret cult but one that is open to all and there is no series of semi-divine beings between us and God. Iconoclasm was rejected because the invisible has made himself visible in Christ. In contrast to Judaism and Islam, for Christians it is important to have icons that witness to the truth of the incarnation. It is not always easy at the time to discern whether a particular development (such as the ordination of women) is one that is in accord with the identity of the whole or whether it changes it. But this is no different from the discussions, sometimes passionate, that go on in literature and all the arts about what is a genuine work of art when it is very different from what has been counted such in the past. The same qualities of patient discernment, rational reflection and judgement are required. The Christian tradition has exhibited extraordinary richness and vitality in the way it has related to different ages and cultures. This is a mark of its strength not a weakness.

Science, like religion, uses metaphors and models and these develop in particular historical settings. For example, most of us do not think that our character traits are due to the constellation of stars at the time of our birth. We look instead to the language of the geneticist. This has been forged in a particular tradition of investigation and a context of agreement about what constitutes evidence and what is a genuine argument. Scientific theories, whilst they set out to depict reality, also develop in particular contexts, both historical and cultural. So as Janet Martin Soskice has put it, arguing that whilst both science and religion use metaphors, in neither case does this stop them legitimately seeking to depict reality.

> The models used will inevitably be linked to particular historical and social contexts. On my argument this isn't a vice but the very foundation of the realist case: having a shared descriptive vocabulary in a tradition is one's only chance of being able to say anything at all, in Theology, Science, Ethics, or any other field of interest and endeavour. A shared and mature descriptive vocabulary gives the possibility of sustained reflection which goes beyond the necessarily limited experiences of each individual.[13]

When a person enters a Benedictine monastery as a novice, they become part of a tradition that has been going for more than 1,400 years. On the basis of the relatively short Rule drawn up by Benedict a way of life has developed which has sustained monastic communities in every age and almost every country. No doubt the Rule has been interpreted somewhat differently by different generations, some parts have been given greater prominence at some times. But it is the continuity of the life which is overwhelming, the identity over so many centuries and cultures. What is true of the Benedictine life is true of the life of the Church as a whole, allowing for the fact that a much greater diversity has to be held together.

The true God seeks to make his purpose known. He has done this in the life of the people of Israel, through the struggles and anguish of their history, as reflected in the Hebrew Scriptures. He does this in Christ, as that history comes to a focus, and in the community that gathered round the risen, ascended and glorified Lord, as reflected in the pages of the New Testament. In the fourth century, the Canon of the New Testament was closed off. Some books were judged to be in and others out. But the closing of the Canon in the fourth century should not close our eyes to the real continuity that exists between the community of Christians today and the community of Christians in every age right down to those first disciples. The fact that what we have apprehended of God's mind and purpose has always been expressed in human terms and arises in a particular historical context does not of itself mean that there is no real God thus disclosing himself. Nor does the fact that Christian belief has been expressed in different ways in different ages and different cultures mean that there is no essential Christian identity. On the contrary, Christian identity, through continuous change, is remarkably striking. To take one simple and obvious example. Jesus lived his life orientated towards the one he called 'Abba', 'Father'. He did this in a relation of sonship, filled by the Holy Spirit. This is beautifully pictured in the account of the Baptism of Christ where the Father says, 'This is my beloved Son in whom I am well pleased' and the Holy Spirit is present symbolized as a dove. Through Christ Christians come to share in the same relationship to God that Christ eternally enjoys and which he incarnated. Through our faith and baptism we too come to relate to God as Father. We too share in Christ's relationship of sonship to God. We too are filled with the Holy Spirit. Nor of course is this relationship a private one even though it may properly be intensely personal. This is the faith of the Church, this is how the Church in its liturgy and worship relates to God, and our personal faith takes on this character through our membership of the Church. Christianity is not frightened of the historical. On the contrary, Christians believe that God has disclosed himself in a special, unique way in a particular person in a particular culture and at a particular time. This 'scandal of particularity' is something our minds jib at. But it is another aspect of a God prepared to be vulnerable. For God has not only put himself at the mercy of events in history, he has put himself at the mercy of historians (and all of us who read the Bible) as we try to reconstruct those events and their meaning.

The question whether religious language refers to a real God, or whether it is simply the expression of our own moral values and ideals may remain. What is beyond question is that throughout Christian history, Christians have thought that their language referred to a real God, one who was truly there and not just a projection of their own wishes or fears. I have argued that the fact that all Christian beliefs have a historical context and are spoken or written by human beings cannot be taken to show that such beliefs are simply made up by human beings. On the contrary, the continuity is an impressive witness to Christian identity, whilst the varying emphases and differences of expression are what should be expected from a living tradition.

Chapter 4

RELATING TO REALITY

Anthony Freeman no longer believes in what he calls a supernatural God. This is a slightly tendentious term, with its overtones of magic. I should prefer to use the more traditional phrase and refer to a transcendent God. In any case he thinks that all 'God talk' refers to human values and ideals. As indicated in the last chapter he arrives at this conclusion because of the inevitable historical context of our beliefs and the obvious presence of human factors in their formulation. Everything seems to him to be slippery, sliding and relative. Because each generation seems to have its own interpretation of the faith, he feels free to adopt his own, one which is expressed in purely human terms. So he writes: 'Observations made within the natural world can give us no information beyond the natural world.' He finds disbelief in a transcendent God a liberating experience because not only does it relieve a sense of oppression, but he is excited at the possibility of discovering within himself new images and metaphors. 'I find myself on a voyage of discovery, creating new maps.' The issue then is whether human language can refer to a transcendent reality or not.

Although Freeman does not spell this out in his short book, behind his position lies the ethos of the 'Sea of Faith' group which might be called a post-modernist or deconstructionist attitude to religion.

This approach could be said to begin with the simple observation that mind is a social reality and language a public phenomenon. We see mothers bending over their prams making noises at their babies. In due course the noises are reciprocated and come to be recognized as talk. Soon this talk becomes internalized as thought. But the talk is prior and public and this enters into the very soul of our thinking. Because language is a public possession, written texts are particularly important. How those texts are interpreted or read still depends very much on the interests and outlook of the readers and these in turn will reflect the interests and concerns already built into the language that we use to interpret the texts. If we say we want to find out what a particular text really means, we are stymied, for the language we use to interpret it ourselves is a given, which will shape how we read. Moreover the text itself will be an interpretation of other texts. So what we have are interpretations of interpretations of interpretations. We cannot get behind a text to the author and find out what he really meant by writing it. All we can do is read the text itself critically, watching with suspicion for the hidden interests or purposes that might be expressed in it and then engage in a creative interplay with the text, an almost playful interpretation of it in our own terms.[14]

There is much here that Christians can take on board, but not the total scepticism about truth and meaning which this approach to texts implies. If all we have are interpretations of interpretations of interpretations, each one shaped by, if not at the mercy of, the public language of the interpreter, then questions of meaning and truth disappear. Philosophy and theology could no longer exist in any traditional form, for the only concern would be the use which some texts had made of previous ones.

That this general approach lies behind Freeman's view can be seen in the following paragraph where he writes:

A false distinction within Christian doctrine itself between an essential core and a negotiable husk. In presenting the faith to this generation I am bound to be presenting a *different* faith from that which my forefathers presented. Not just a *different interpretation* of the same essential core, but a *different faith*. This is because there is no essence or inner core. The interpretation is not like taking the shell off a nut. It is like peeling the layers off an onion: the interpretation goes all the way down. All is interpretation. That *is* the essence.

Towards the end of the book, Freeman writes:

There are certain fundamental errors about which I feel too strongly to keep quiet ... Foremost among them is precisely

the way we feel ourselves bound to the past! And linked
with this, we do need to get away from the idea that there is
somewhere an unchanging hard-core of 'the faith'.

These passages at once reveal a fatal flaw, one column to all
forms of extreme scepticism about the possibility of attaining an
objective truth. For the statement that all is interpretation, 'The
interpretation goes all the way down', is, in his view, itself an
interpretation and therefore cannot claim to be the truth. Despite
this, Freeman often appeals to what he believes to be true. He
writes of 'a false distinction within Christian doctrine itself' and
that 'there are certain fundamental errors'. To talk about false
distinctions and fundamental errors implies that it is possible to
distinguish between what is true and false, between what is
accurate and what is in error. This itself presupposes that it is
possible to reach agreement and that not everything is interpretation. To use the jargon for a moment, Freeman himself is open
to deconstruction, one which points to the truth he is trying to
demolish.

In recent years historians, particularly in America, have
become acutely conscious that history is always written from a
particular point of view. We now have history from the
standpoint of black people, of women, of Jews, Hispanics,
Catholics and so on. This has led some people to think that it is
impossible to attain objective truths about any episode in history,
and to a total relativism. Yet there are already signs that this
crisis (which has never been prevalent amongst historians in
Britian) is passing. For as one distinguished historian has put it:

> One representation of the past is not as good as another, for
> the documents and material remains are there to be
> consulted and checked by fellow historians; the experiment
> can be replicated and errors exposed. It is therefore not
> difficult to discriminate between competing accounts of
> past reality.[15]

History has always been a continuing interaction between the
present and the past. We are rightly much more aware than our
forebears of how the present affects the way we reconstruct the
past. But this does not mean it is impossible to reach agreement

about an incident or period in history or, in Christian terms, what the faith might have meant to people in the eighteenth, fourteenth or fourth centuries. I now want to look more closely at the two passages quoted.

These passages are concerned with the relationship between Christian truth and the different cultures in which it has been set and taught. It is important to note that in exploring this relationship we will inevitably use metaphors, analogies and pictures. And metaphors, of their nature, can only fasten on a limited number of features that the two things being compared have in common. They are therefore always as untrue as they are true, and this is so of all use of metaphor, not only when applied to God. So when Freeman and others talk about the relationship between the Christian faith and its expression in a particular culture as like that between 'an essential core and a negotiable husk', this analogy, if it applies at all, will be both helpful and misleading. Freeman rejects it altogether. There is, however, some truth in it. In the last chapter I pointed out that the continuities in Christian sensibility are as striking as the discontinuities; our sense of association with the past is as marked as our consciousness of dissociation. It is genuinely possible to enter into the outlook and faith of past Christians and sometimes to feel very close to them. This of itself indicates that there is something in the 'core' analogy. But I wish to take an example from another field of study to show how there can be real persistence in time, through very different societies, of certain fundamentals.

Francesco de Vitoria was a sixteenth-century Spanish Dominican. He was appalled by the way the Spanish were treating the native Indians in South America and wrote a book condemning certain kinds of atrocity. In it he lays down certain moral principles, for example that women and children should never be the direct object of attack, even in a war which is morally justified. Vitoria's book has been important both for ethics and law. In particular the principle of discrimination, that those not directly contributing to a war effort should never be the direct object of attack, has been to the fore in a number of modern debates. The circumstances have been very different. For example, in a guerrilla warfare, what about women who carry grenades concealed in their clothing? If ammunition workers are a legitimate object of attack and bakers are not, because they are not directly contributing to the war effort but providing bread for the civilian population as a whole, what about those who make military uniforms? In a world bristling with nuclear weapons, can such weapons legitimately be targeted on military installations near cities? The circumstances have been different and those circumstances may pose new questions but the principle that though civilians do of course, tragically, suffer in a war, they should not be attacked directly unless they are in a direct way aiding the military machine, has been widely accepted. It has passed not only into international law but into the military law of most countries. However often it has been violated, it is recognized as an abiding principle. This is a 'core' that has not only persisted but which has in fact established itself even more strongly through all its different applications. What holds good for an ethical and legal principle can also apply to the fundamental tenets of a religion.

The core/husk analogy, like all analogies, is of limited use. It inevitably fails in a number of ways. For example, the Christian faith is not static, like the kernel of a nut. It has grown, adapted and developed. Cardinal Newman, when an Anglican, compared Christian truth to a wide flowing river that had originally emerged from a muddy spring. Close to the spring it is difficult to tell what is fresh water and what is mud. By the time the stream has become a river however it is much more clear what Christian truth is and stands for. Or we might take the analogy of a tree. A tree weathers in response to its environment. It may bend because of a prevailing wind. It is affected by the quality of the soil, the amount of sunshine, whether other trees are growing around it, whether it is attacked by fungi or insects, or whether it is pruned. Yet the full-grown tree is the same tree as the sapling from which it sprung.

Freeman compares the faith of different generations to peeling an onion. One layer after another comes off until nothing is left. There is no essence or inner core. Yet, as each layer is peeled off, you still have an onion, the same onion. The colour may be different, the size and weight are certainly different. But there is a fundamental continuity. The smell, taste, texture and structure are the same. You can let the onion sprout and then replant it. It will produce seeds that if planted in their turn will produce onions: onions with a genetic resemblance to the one from which they came. Christianity can be planted and grown in very different cultures. But a family likeness remains.

Earlier I referred to Jesus' relationship to God as a son to a father. I was taught to pray to God in the words 'Our Father, who art in heaven'. No doubt from the first I have made my own interpretation of that, as my mother did before me, and her mother did before her, going back through Christian history to Paul who wrote:

> When we cry 'Abba! Father!' it is the Spirit himself bearing witness with our spirit that we are children of God. (Romans 8.15)

Behind that is Jesus who himself prayed to God as Abba, Father, and taught his followers to do the same. I believe that when I pray to God as Father, what I mean is essentially what Jesus meant, namely that there is a wise and loving power behind human existence, whom I can trust utterly. This claim may be true or false. The point is that as we peel off the layers, a similar structure remains. Or, to take up the other aspect of the analogy, the seeds of Christ's faith will produce a faith resembling the faith from which the seeds came. We come back to the faith of Jesus – and, I would argue, to the Jewish tradition which shaped and nurtured his whole understanding of God.

There is another way of looking at this issue and that is in relation to the question of personal identity. Am I the same person now that I was at age 7, 17, 27, 37 etc. We are told that the cells of our body are totally changed every few years. I look different, I may feel different. Apart from genetic identification, similarity of DNA, is there any way within myself that I know I am the same person? Our memory is one indication. I have memories, say, of holidays at the seaside as a child. My memories indicate that I was once that child. The Church too has memories; indeed there is a profound sense in which it lives on its memories. At the Last Supper Jesus told his followers to do certain things in rememb-rance of him and the Church in every age and in every culture has done just that. Whether the outward form has been elaborate as in a High Mass, or simple, a small gathering round a table, it is Jesus who is remembered. As the acclamation in the Eucharist puts it:

> Christ has died:
> Christ is risen:
> Christ will come again.

That acclamation indicates that Christian memories are integrally bound up with Christian hopes. Jesus looked for the coming of God's Kingdom and so did the writers of the New Testament and so do we. Indeed, Christian memories are not of the dead past, but anticipations of a new future. In Jesus that ultimate state of affairs, in which God's love will overcome all obstacles, was anticipated and made present. So when the Church remembers Jesus, we too are anticipating and making present that ultimate state of affairs. As to be human is .to have memories and hopes, so the Church's identity, in every age and every culture, is shaped by its memories which are at the same time the ground of the hopes.

The American theologian Paul Tillich said that each age had its own particular anxiety from which the Christian faith can deliver us. In the world of the first Christians, this was above all the sense of fate, the feeling that everything is governed by implacable, impersonal forces, for example, the planets. During the late medieval and early Reformation period it was above all a sense of guilt which beset and burdened people. In our own time, Tillich argues, it is a sense of lostness and meaninglessness from which we suffer. Freeman seems to accept a similar kind of historical pattern and so do I. It is vitally important that the Christian faith be communicated to people in a way that really does speak to and meet their needs. So it is that Christian life takes multiple forms. In India the faith can be expressed in and through the extraordinary vitality and beauty of classical Hindu dance. In Soweto it can be expressed with all the warm human exuberance and joy of a community conscious of belonging with one another, not apart from one another. In Latin America it can be expressed in communities committed to the poor and characterized by a real sharing of life and goods. The richness and diversity of forms of Christian life and witness are part of its strength. Moreover it is not just cultures that differ. Each of us has our own particular needs and these vary at different times in our lives. It may be that the Christian hope of eternal life will speak to a person who is old in a way that it does not to a teenager. Conversely, it may be that the Christian claim to offer true life, life with a capital 'L', authentic and abundant life, will mean something to that teenager in a way that it may not to someone who is in a mid-life crisis.

The Church has always claimed that the Christian faith is good news. In order for it to be good news rather than stale or bad news, it needs to meet the actual needs of particular people, where they are. As the preface to the Declaration of Assent used by the Anglican Church puts it, Christ is to be 'proclaimed afresh in every generation'. For there to be this freshness, there must be a real sensitivity to people's needs and a genuine creativity in seeking to speak to and respond to them.

People sometimes make the mistake of hankering after a single formula, in which the Christian faith can be encapsulated. But the Gospel is not a slogan. When Mahler's Sixth Symphony was first performed the composer was prevailed upon to write some programme notes for it, setting out its 'meaning'. He did this, but bitterly regretted having done so, saying that such attempts to sum up a complex piece of music in a few words have a 'coarsening effect'. The same might be said of attempts to say what a particular poem 'means'. This may sometimes be necessary for teaching purposes, but a poem is a poem; its meaning is in the particular assembly of words and sounds. When a person has made the Christian faith their own and they talk about it in a natural way to a friend, or even when they speak about it in public, their words will have something in common with music or a poem. Through thought and prayer it will have become deeply part of their own experience and being. What they communicate will therefore have a unique quality to it, as does any true poem. There will be creativity in it, not necessarily in any high artistic sense, but drawing on the creative potential which is in all of us to feel and see things in a special way. So when it comes to sharing the Christian faith or witnessing to it, let a thousand flowers bloom, and let each one be different.

However, this good news which is shared will be quarried from a Christian tradition with, as I have argued, a recognizable identity. To quote the preface to the Declaration of Assent again, the Church 'professes the faith uniquely revealed in the Holy Scriptures and set forth in the Catholic Creeds'.

Any Christian worthy of the name will be as passionate as Anthony Freeman about wanting to help proclaim the faith 'afresh in each generation' and will want to share in 'bringing the grace and truth of Christ to this generation'. But the Christian faith we seek to set forth in fresh ways is the faith of the Church, the faith uniquely revealed in the Holy Scriptures and set forth in the Catholic creeds, to which the historical formularies of all Christian denominations seek to bear witness in their different ways.

I hope enough has been said here to show that we are not simply at the mercy of successive layers of interpretation. Questions about meaning and truth still have validity. We are not simply a conduit through which the language of our society passes. We are actors, using language in particular contexts to say and do particular things. We are shaped by this language but not totally determined by it.

We can, further, get behind texts to the author and ask what the author might have meant. Through Paul's Letters to the Corinthians for example we can build up a picture of the church in Corinth and what Paul was trying to say to it. Paul, the church in Corinth, and the Church throughout the ages, like the Church today, uses language to refer to a real God, a transcendent reality, not just a personification of our ideas and ideals.

All language about God is ineradicably metaphorical. But this does not mean that it cannot refer to a real God. It is important to note however that we should beware of referring to 'mere metaphor'. Metaphors are ways of speaking. The truth or falsity of what is asserted is not settled and cannot be settled simply by the fact that metaphor is used. If I say about someone that they are 'bursting with energy', this is a metaphorical way of speaking. But the fact that I have used a metaphor to describe this person does not affect whether what I say is true or false. Whether they are in fact like this will be judged on how much they do, how quickly they do it, when they get tired and so on. It is not untrue because the metaphor 'bursting' is used. Similarly when the Jesus of the Fourth Gospel says 'I am the vine and you are the branches', it is obvious that this is metaphorical. But the fact that a metaphor is used cannot of itself tell us whether the claim is true or false. It has to be judged on other grounds. Then, as Janet Martin Soskice has argued, science also uses models and metaphors in order to explore the nature of reality, even before a definite description of that reality can be given. People sometimes hanker after a clear, non-metaphorical assertion about God, to which all metaphors can be applied. This cannot come about because everything we say about God involves metaphor. Yet, as in the use of metaphors in science, we can still make definite claims which will in due course turn out to be true or false or perhaps in need of some qualification.

Janet Martin Soskice rejects the word reality-description and prefers the phrase reality-depiction, for what metaphors in science and religion are seeking to do. As far as religion is concerned, I prefer the term reality-relating. I cannot depict God as he is. However, through the use of appropriate metaphors and pictures I can be related rightly to God. I can come to respond, to trust, to hope. Of course, there must be some relationship between relating to reality and depicting it. I only come to put my trust in God if I believe that in some profound sense God is trustworthy or faithful. So metaphors do need to point, truthfully, to some aspect of God. Nevertheless their purpose is not primarily to depict, but to relate us rightly to God.

Chapter 5

HE LIVED AND DIED
AND ROSE AGAIN FOR US

In his chapter on Jesus, Freeman again takes up the theme that the way the Christian faith has been stated varies enormously from age to age. In the first centuries the proclamation of the faith focused on the gift of immortality, which Christ renews. In the medieval and Reformation period, it centred on forgiveness of sin and deliverance from hell. I hope I have said enough in the previous chapters to show that different emphases or ways of stating the faith in no way imply that it is simply the product of each age, a human invention. In fact the themes to which he refers, the gifts of immortality and forgiveness of sins, are not mutually exclusive. They both relate to the Christian faith as rooted in Jesus and spelt out by the Church.

Freeman then carries his argument into the New Testament itself, saying that the picture of Jesus we get in the different writings varies enormously and each one reflects a particular faith or point of view. People often make a distinction between the Jesus of history and the Christ of faith. But that distinction no longer holds, for the gospels are written from the standpoint of faith. With all this I agree. But once again illegitimate conclusions are drawn.

One conclusion is that it is now impossible to get behind the Christ of faith to reconstruct any picture of Jesus in his historical setting. Albert Schweitzer accused writers of the lives of Jesus in the nineteenth century of looking down the long well of history and seeing their own faces reflected at the bottom. Freeman believes that this will always be the case, that we will always simply reconstruct a Jesus in the image of ourselves or our own age.

Although I am not a New Testament scholar, he is I think somewhat out of touch here in his total scepticism about

recovering a historically accurate picture of Jesus. It is true that
the first quest for the historical Jesus served only to reveal the
subjective bias of the writers and that the second quest can only
come up with minimal results. Nevertheless, there is a second
quest, engaged in by a wide range of reputable scholars, Jewish
as well as Christian, and there is agreement on many points.[16] It
might also be noticed that classical scholars and others who
work on ancient documents usually accuse New Testament
scholars of being over sceptical. One can understand why that
might be so. In any case, even with an extreme degree of
scepticism, with the most rigorous tests of what might be
historically accurate, a particular picture of Jesus in his Jewish
context has emerged.

It is of course always open to Freeman or anyone else to say
that in a hundred years time the present generation of scholars
will also be accused of simply reflecting their own age and, of
course, there will be something of our age in the picture of Jesus
they produce. History is always an unending dialogue between
the present and the past, so that future generations are always in
the business of correcting the historical reconstructions of their
forebears. But at least our generation is aware of the danger, and
reputable scholars do what they can to counteract this tendency.
Moreover we can see in our own time a clear difference between
those lives of Jesus which obviously reflect a subjective
viewpoint and those which are the result of patient, objective
scholarship. In recent years we have been inundated with so-
called lives of Jesus, painting the most extraordinary pictures:
from Jesus as the founder of a cult of hallucinogenic mushroom
eaters, to a kind of ancient Che Guevara, via Jesus as a Hindu
guru figure and so on. Such pictures create a furore in the papers
for a day or two and then go the way of all trash. When there
may be something in a particular thesis, as there was some
possibility in the idea of a relationship between Jesus and the
Zealot movement of his time (a thesis which was very popular in
the 1960s), then patient scholarship is able to correct the
distortions and establish a truer historical record. Freeman's total
scepticism about the Jesus of history is unwarranted. We can
reconstruct the main outlines of the life and teaching of Jesus
with as much certainty as we can have about any historical
knowledge. Freeman goes beyond this historical scepticism,

however, when he says that it simply 'does not matter' whether
or not we can find out anything about Jesus. 'Who needs a
historical Jesus?' He maintains that the New Testament writers,
like all of us, simply create the kind of Christ of faith we want
anyway.

We do all of course to some extent picture Jesus in our own
terms. In Nazareth there is a large modern Roman Catholic
church which has pictures of Jesus and his early life from almost
every culture in the world. Indian, Japanese, Philippine, African
and other artists depict Jesus in ways which can be recognized
and appreciated by their own culture. This is as it should be. But
it does not follow that there is no true record of the historical
Jesus or that we can sit light to that record. It matters that Jesus
lived and it matters that we can know, at least in outline, what he
said and did, because in him the life of God is made accessible
in human terms. So there needs to be a likeness, or congruity,
between what he said, how he lived and what the Church
believes is revealed about God in and through him. I take two
examples.

Jesus mixed with and ate with those beyond the pale of
respectable religious society. The fact that he shared table
fellowship with such people, a very special sign of intimacy and
friendship, in particular aroused criticism. In response Jesus told
stories like the one about the woman who scrabbled all over the
floor to find a lost coin or a shepherd who scoured the hills for a
lost sheep. Moreover he said that the Kingdom of God, the
activity of God himself, is like that. God goes out of the way to
bring the lost home. In short, what Jesus did and what he taught
about God's Kingdom have the same pattern or character, they
are of a piece. If today we claim that God is a God who always
reaches out to us, however much we may hide away or feel we
have disqualified ourselves from his favour, it is in large
measure because of what Jesus taught us, the pattern of his
earthly life, and what his whole life, death and resurrection came
to mean to the first Christians. This leads into the second
example. The fact that Jesus was crucified is one of the best
attested facts of history. Of course people can question whether
this actually happened, as they can question anything and
everything. Enoch Powell has recently questioned even the
crucifixion, but most scholars would say that if we know

anything at all about the past, we know that Jesus of Nazareth was crucified under Pontius Pilate.

The central theme of the teaching of Jesus was what he called the Kingdom of God, the just and gentle rule of God in human affairs. All the way through the Hebrew Scriptures, people long for God to act in this world to put right everything that is wrong. The writers were conscious, as we are, that so often injustice is done, the poor are oppressed and the innocent suffer. They believed and hoped there would come a time when all this would stop, when God would establish his just rule over the kingdoms of the earth. It was about this Kingdom that Jesus taught. It was this he proclaimed as in some sense already present or breaking into human life. He opened his mission with the theme: 'Repent and believe, the Kingdom of God is at hand.' In other words, rethink your whole life, reorientate yourself towards God and live even now in his presence, under his just and gentle rule. Jesus literally lived for this Kingdom. But he died an apparent failure, abandoned by his followers, denied by his closest intimate, perhaps even doubting himself: 'My God, my God, why hast thou forsaken me?' Was he totally mistaken? Was it all an illusion? After the first shock of the crucifixion was over the first followers of Jesus, in a wave of realization, came to think that he was *not* mistaken, that in some profound sense the rule of God in human history had begun to dawn, not in a way that was obvious to the world as a whole, but in Jesus himself. For they claimed that he had been raised by God from the dead. The tomb was found empty and a number of his followers claimed to have encountered him, in his risen form. They still looked forward to the time when the Kingdom of God would come in its fullness but it was now, a Kingdom defined in terms of Jesus and one they believed had in some profound sense already been established in him. Through the life, death and resurrection of Jesus, God had acted. In him the mighty had been put down from their seats and the humble and meek had been exalted. In the person of Jesus, the poor, those who put their total trust in God, the innocent, the oppressed, were vindicated, were raised to the right hand of God for ever. Henceforth the first would be last and the last first. Whereas the message of Jesus was about the Kingdom of God, the message of the first followers of Jesus after the resurrection was no less about Jesus himself. For in him

the Kingdom had dawned, and through him the Kingdom would
be consummated.

I am not for the moment concerned with the truth or falsity of
this claim, simply with the unmistakable implication that it turns
on certain historical facts: that Jesus lived, that he proclaimed
the Kingdom of God and its coming, and that in some serious
but real way God's presence and rule was indeed in Jesus.

Freeman sees Jesus as a focus for our human values and
ideals. But Jesus was not simply an ethical teacher. His teaching
was nearly always related to living in God's Kingdom, with
certain clear implications about his own role in relation to that
Kingdom. It is not possible to take Jesus seriously without
reckoning with these claims. For Jesus lived his whole life
towards the one he called 'Abba, Father'. He put his whole trust
in him. Against all human inclinations and instincts he went
through with his mission, in the belief that this is what he had to
do. 'Father, take this cup from me, nevertheless not my will but
thine be done.' Yet Jesus was crucified. The Kingdom did not
seem to have come. Was it all a terrible illusion? The Church
came to think that Jesus was right because of the resurrection. I
realize of course that this presents major difficulties. Some
people who are able to believe in God, and who respond to the
major tenets of the teachings of Jesus, just find it impossible to
believe that he was raised from the dead. But the teaching of
Jesus, taken with the fact of the crucifixion, makes it clear that a
great deal hangs on this. There is no way in which we can avoid
the centrality of the claim that Jesus was raised from the dead,
however much we would like to sidle round it. For the
crucifixion called all that Jesus stood for into question.
Moreover because what Jesus stood for was total trust in a
totally trustworthy power behind this world, it also calls all that
into question. Nothing less is at stake than the Church's central
message, that there is a God and that this God is one of
undeviating goodwill towards us. The Church invites us to put
our whole trust in God, as Jesus did. Whether we are able to do
so or not depends in large measure on what we think happened
'on the third day'. There is no way in which we can side-step the
crucial significance of certain historical claims, that Jesus lived,
that he die, and that he was raised to a universal
contemporaneity, so that he is present with us now as God is

present, a human focus of the eternal, invisible one.[17]

Freeman believes that if we see Jesus as simply a focus for our human ideals, this will make it much easier for Christianity to relate to other religions in a peaceful way. Without any claim that God is real, without any claim that Jesus is a unique disclosure of this God, Christianity would no longer be a threat to other religions and if they adopted the same approach towards religious truth, they would no longer be a threat to Christians. All religious statements would be seen as expressions of human values, some of them shared with adherents of other religions, and some particular to each tradition. But followers of each tradition would recognize that other traditions have values that are no less valid for them.

This approach is, however, useless as a way of bringing about greater religious understanding and tolerance, for the fact is that Jews, Muslims, Sikhs and many others do believe, believe passionately, that God is real and has a purpose for us. Moreover they are not interested in any form of discussion which involves discarding or watering down of central beliefs as a precondition for dialogue.

The 1988 Lambeth Conference brought out a document, *Jews, Muslims and Christians: the Way of Dialogue*,[18] which set out three fundamental principles: the way of understanding, so that we try to understand other religions in their terms, rather than through our stereotypes; the way of affirmation, exploring and affirming all possible ground in common; the way of sharing. This last means that all participants to dialogue will bring to it their fundamental convictions and on the basis of mutual respect there will be a sharing. If there has been a genuine attempt to see the other religion as it is through their eyes, and if it has been possible to affirm some beliefs and attitudes in common, then it is quite possible to have a mutual sharing of beliefs even when they radically differ. Indeed this last element is essential if the dialogue is to be a genuine meeting and not simply a polite avoidance of the real issues. I believe that dialogue of this kind is essential for all religions and that it is also possible. Freeman's view is a fantasy that bears no relation at all to the actualities of interfaith relationships today.

In this chapter I have argued that it is possible to reconstruct the main outlines of the life and teaching of Jesus, and that this matters. It matters because Jesus was not just a teacher of human ideals. He taught about the Kingdom of God and the impact of this resulted in him being crucified. This rejection calls into question all that he stood for, including his faith in a loving God. Much therefore depends on whether we can believe that God vindicated his trust by raising him from the dead. It is very awkward that the Christian faith is committed to certain historical facts. But these facts make the Christian religion what it is. Adherents of other religions expect Christians to take these beliefs with them when they enter into dialogue and would not respect them if they laid them aside in the vain hope of an easy religious harmony.

Chapter 6

TRUE GOD TRULY IN US

Freeman holds that the Church has too long been in the business of keeping God and human beings apart from one another. The coming of the Holy Spirit should have bridged that gap for everyone for all time. As the prophet Jeremiah had put it: 'No longer shall each man teach his neighbour and each his brother saying, "Know the Lord, For they shall know me, from the least of them to the greatest", saith the Lord' (Jeremiah 31.34). In fact, what happened, he alleges, is that organized religion once again took over and controlled the gap. It only allowed the Holy Spirit to reach people through the sacraments and teaching of the Church. Freeman's view is that there is no real God, and therefore no gap. We should take the presence of the Holy Spirit within all of us as a symbol of our own creative human powers. 'It is precisely by looking towards what is noblest and best in our human spirit that we should discover the Holy Spirit shed abroad in our hearts.' Through engaging in activities of social and political reform and doing good in our own personal lives, we discover and express that 'holy human spirit'.

Before responding to Freeman, I will sketch out what a traditional view of the Holy Spirit might look like. I refer again to the picture or icon of the Baptism of Jesus himself. In the centre of the picture is Jesus being baptized. From the Father come the words, 'This is my beloved Son in whom I am well pleased'. The Holy Spirit symbolized as a dove rests upon him. This is a picture of the truths in which Jesus exercised his ministry. His life was directed to the Father but it was filled and guided by that Spirit. Indeed, the Church believes that this icon is a working out in human terms of what is eternally true of God himself. Within the eternal Godhead, the Father gives himself everlastingly to the Son, who responds with a perfect reciprocity of love, whilst the Holy Spirit, love itself, circles between them, proceeding from the Father and filling the Son. This is only a picture and some may not find it helpful. The essential point is that Jesus, as understood by the Church, did not see his ministry in relation to God the Father alone. His life was one that was lived from the Spirit within him. What is so wonderful is that Christians, through their faith and baptism, receive the gift of that same Spirit. In and through Christ we too relate to God as Father and we too are filled with the same Spirit which filled Jesus. In short, we might simply say that the Holy Spirit is God within us. This is not an understanding of God that has been made up in our own time, it is thoroughly biblical. It is there in Paul and there in John. In the dialogues in John's gospel, Jesus a number of times says to his followers that God will come to dwell in them. If they obey his fundamental command, which is to love one another, then God will dwell with them and in them.

So God is not only beyond us and about us but within us. Moment by moment God holds us in being. Without his creating, sustaining power as the ground of all being, we would simply dissolve into nothingness. But that which holds us in being, seeks to fill us with himself, to become the spring flowing up within us, the source from which our life is lived. Indeed Jesus tells the woman at Jacob's well that the water he will give her, water being a symbol for the Holy Spirit, will be a spring welling up within her for eternal life.

The teaching that God is not only beyond all things but within all things has not always received the emphasis it should. But it has certainly been present in the Christian mystical tradition. In that tradition, we are urged to know the centre of our centre, the soul of our soul, for there God above all is to be discovered. As Julian of Norwich wrote:

> Our soul is so deep grounded in God so endlessly treasured, that we may not come to the knowing thereof until we have, first, knowing of God, who is the maker; to whom it is oned. But notwithstanding I saw that we have, of our fullness the desire wisely and truly to know our own soul, whereby we are learned to seek it where it is, and that is, in God.[19]

In the modern world there is great stress on the individual self, on the importance of discovering ourselves, of being true to

ourselves and fulfilling ourselves. There is nothing wrong with
the Church taking this as the starting-point for its sharing of the
Gospel. But we will begin by asking some critical questions, not
only how we are to find this fulfilment or in what it should
consist, but what is this self? What is the self which we are to
discover, express and fulfil? It is not simply the product of our
genetic inheritance or our childhood influences. Our true self is
discovered as we rest in and live from the God who dwells
within us, the Holy Spirit. Insofar as we are able to rest in and
live from the deepest centre of our being, the point at which the
divine spring bubbles up, we will be the self we are created to
be.

In one of his finest poems Gerard Manley Hopkins pictures
everything in nature being itself (author's italics):

> Each mortal thing does one thing and the same:
> Deals out that being indoors each one dwells;
> Selves – goes itself; *myself* it speaks and spells,
> Crying *what I do is me: for that I came.*

But what about us human beings? What is it for us to be
ourselves? Hopkins goes on to say that the just person, the
person who acts in God's grace:

> Acts in God's eye what in God's eye he is –
>   Christ.
> For Christ plays in ten thousand places,
> Lovely in limbs, and lovely in eyes not his
> To the Father through the features of men's faces.[20]

One of the reasons why the Church has perhaps been
suspicious of the idea that God dwells within us and has
underplayed it is that it is so easy for this to become distorted.
Some, for example, have so emphasized the indwelling of God
in all things, his immanence, that they have lost all sight of
God's otherness, his transcendence. Some indeed have made
God's presence in nature identical with nature itself, so that the
word God has been evacuated of all meaning. One point must be
made crystal clear. God can only fill all things if he is first other
than all things. If God were simply another name for nature, then

it is difficult to see what would be filling what. But if God is the creative ground of all being, the source from which every constituent part of the universe moment by moment springs, then it is possible to say that this same God not only holds all things in existence, but knows all things from within.

The God who is in us is therefore not simply a focus of our human creativity and capacity for good. He is the true God, who is we might say more real than we are ourselves, because he is the source of the reality we have. Given this, however, it is not only possible – it is essential – to affirm that God is truly in us. This is I believe particularly important for people today, when so many do find any concept of God's transcendence, or fatherhood, not simply difficult to believe in but, like Anthony Freeman, oppressive. Father Harry Williams was one person who found the traditional concept of God inimical to his human striving. But he came through to a new experience of God's indwelling. God is, he wrote:

> The fount or source from which we continually flow ...
> God can be described as the ocean of which I am a wave,
> the sun of which I am a shaft of light, the tree of which I
> am a branch.[21]

That last image is of course a biblical one. 'I am the vine, you are the branches' (John 15.5). This parallels Paul's statement that 'I live, yet not I but Christ in me' (Galatians 2.20).

This means that it may very well be important for people in their own spiritual life, for periods, even long periods, to focus exclusively upon God within them rather than the God beyond or about them. Many have found the traditional prayer from the 1558 Sarum Primer helpful for this purpose. Said slowly, in a reflective manner with lots of silence, it can help to centre us, to rest in and live from that deepest point within us, the point at which the Holy Spirit touches and quickens us.

> God be in my head and in my understanding;
> God be in my eyes and in my looking;
> God be in my mouth, and in my speaking;
> God be in my heart and in my thinking;
> God be at mine end, and at my departing.

Chapter 7

LIFE WITH GOD FOR EVER

Freeman rightly points out in his chapter 'Now is eternal life', that there are many different pictures in the Bible and Christian tradition of what happens to us after death. I have already argued that different ways of stating Christian truth in different ages does not of itself undermine the idea that there can be continuity and a persistent Christian identity. I will simply state my understanding of the Christian hope. First, it *is* about hope – not only for oneself but for the whole world. The German theologian Jurgen Moltmann, who is passionately concerned about changing conditions on this earth, can still ask whether as Christians we can have hope in the face of death. The answer is yes. We may be totally agnostic about the way in which that hope is to be fulfilled. We may admit to knowing nothing at all about conditions in the afterlife. But we can still have hope as we approach our own end and as we contemplate the death of those we love.

Second, if asked to sketch out this hope a little more I would say that my true self, who I really am, is known to God and he can re-create it in the form appropriate to an eternal existence. Who we really are is something of a mystery. We can never know ourselves fully. But God knows us through and through. Furthermore, although our knowledge of things may appear to end with death, God's knowledge of me does not. Who I truly am is known and kept within the heart of the eternal God who will, in faith and hope, give me another form of expression.[22] When Dietrich Bonhoeffer was in prison he wrote a moving poem called 'Who am I?' In it he describes how other people thought of him as so confident, striding out like a squire from his country house. Yet inside himself, he knew himself to be sick and afraid, lonely and bewildered. He wonders which is his true self, the one others see or the one he knows inside. He ends the poem:

> Who am I? They mock me, these lonely
>   questions of mine.
> Whoever I am, thou knowest, O God, I
>   am thine![23]

Despite all our questioning and doubts, despite the fact that so much is unknown, we can trust that we are known to God and that we belong to him for ever.

In order to share this hope it is not necessary to believe that we have a soul that is a kind of box within a box. Modern science, like the Hebrews of old, stresses that we are psychosomatic unities, body, mind and spirit all bound up together. It may be that 'soul' language is important in drawing attention to our spiritual nature and destiny. But we do not have to believe that soul is an isolatable thing. Nor do we have to believe that our bodies will be raised from the grave like characters in a painting by Stanley Spencer. So far as we know, our bodies decompose, to become part of the earth which in due course is recycled in other ways. However, when we say in the creed that we believe in the resurrection of the body, this is a vitally important symbolic statement. It means that whatever comes after death is a gift of God. As this life is totally dependent upon its givenness by God, so is whatever comes after. We have no right to it. The soul does not automatically live for ever. The phrase resurrection of the body also indicates that whatever comes next, we will be more truly and richly ourselves, not a mere shadow of what we once were, a wisp of smoke. We will be re-created or re-clothed in the 'stuff of glory', whatever that might be, and that glory will include all the beauty and love of the earth. In the same way that music written for one instrument, say a violin, can sometimes be played on other instruments, the music which we are, played on the instruments of flesh and blood in this life, can be played on another instrument in the next. God knows the tune, he has the notes in his mind. We can sound forth again with all that God deems worthy of preserving.

There are a number of reasons for holding this hope, of which I mention only three. First, as human parents will give to their children what they are capable of giving and what is good for them, so God gives in relation to us. He himself is immortal and in his undeviating goodwill towards us, wills us to share his immortality. It is the nature of God to give and he wishes to bestow upon us the gift of eternal life.

Second, those who have begun something of a relationship with God in this life find it difficult to believe that this relationship will end with death. St Paul wrote:

> For I am sure that neither death, nor life ... nor anything else in all creation, will be able to separate us from the love of God in Christ Jesus our Lord. (Romans 8.38, 39)

In saying this, I am not referring simply to one particular relationship with God, for our own may seem very feeble and frail, but the whole sweep of Christian experience including the great saints and mystics, people who have have been intensely aware of the reality of God. If God is real and God is a God of love, it would be very strange if all that came to nothing.

Third, there is the desperate need for an ultimate justice and the promise given in the resurrection of Jesus Christ, that this justice will indeed be established. There is so much suffering and anguish in the world, so much violated innocence, so many lives cut short before they have had any opportunity of fulfilment, so much cruelty. As mentioned earlier, throughout the Hebrew Scriptures there is this great longing that God will act to put right everything that is wrong and establish his just rule in human affairs. The first Christians believed that this kingdom had indeed begun to be established through the life and death and resurrection of Jesus. He is the poor man, the innocent, the one who losing out on this earth nevertheless trusts God to the end, whom God vindicates; in vindicating Jesus, God promises to raise all who stand with him in outraged innocence and rejected goodness. Some people on Easter Sunday think of the festival primarily in terms of proof that there is an afterlife. But Easter is much more that. There could be an afterlife, such as the spiritualists sometimes suggest, which would still have all the flaws of this one. The point about Easter is not only that God in Christ conquers death but that he overcomes all that is hostile to his good purpose.

Since the holocaust, as a result of which 6,000,000 Jews were exterminated, the Jewish community has wrestled with how this terrible event can be reconciled with a belief in a faithful God. Daniel Cohn-Sherbok, in his survey of all the Jewish theological responses to the Shoa, concludes that they all fail because they do not take into account the Jewish hope of everlasting life. It is only by including this in the total picture that it is possible to reconcile such horrifying evil with the claim that there is a good God. More generally, as the Pope's encyclical on liberation theology *Libertas Conscientia* concludes, there is a quest for justice in life that cannot be met until we take into account the hope for eternal life.

> For true justice must include everyone;
> It must bring the answer to the immense load of suffering
> born by all the generations; in fact, without the resurrection
> of the dead and the Lord's judgement, there is no justice in
> the full sense of the term. The promise of the resurrection is
> freely made to meet the desire for true justice dwelling in
> the human heart.

Freeman believes that this desire for true justice can be met by concentrating on the quality of life rather than its extent. He suggests that if we live intensely, in the here and now, in the light of our highest values, then we will achieve a quality of life which is more important than anything else. The quality of a play or poem does not depend on its length, nor does the quality of our lives. There is an important pastoral truth in this. Some years ago when I visited 'The Lighthouse' which had been set up to support AIDS suffers, there was a strong thrust in the work to stop people thinking of themselves as victims. From victim to victor was one slogan that was around. Moving stories were told, as they still are, of people discovering a new quality to their lives in their dying years or months. So this is an important truth. Nevertheless it by no means meets the need for justice for the street children in the cities of Brazil, living in the sewers and shot dead like vermin. It does not meet the need for justice for those Indian brides (more than 5,000 during the last year) killed because the husband's family did not think they brought enough in the way of. It does not meet the need for justice for all those children abused and murdered in the age of innocence. Sadly, these examples could be multiplied endlessly. If there is a loving

God behind this universe, it is difficult to see how he could have brought such lives into existence, to end so shortly and in such pain, without giving them some further opportunity to grow and blossom into the beautiful people that they have within them to be.

This way of thinking could of course be dismissed as wishful thinking, as something which would be very nice if it were true but which is highly unlikely. But if, on other grounds, we already believe in the reality of God, if we believe that he is a God of loving kindness who desires each one of us to grow into the fullness of the stature of Christ, then it is impossible not to believe in a life after death. For the Christian faith has its own inner consistency. There is a logic of love. From the basic premise that there is a God of love ultimately responsible for the world, then certain things inevitably follow. Of course if there is no God, or this God is indifferent or even hostile to human well-being, then the matter is entirely different. But if we believe that God is a God of justice, then we are led inescapably to the conclusion that the establishment of his justice cannot be limited by space and time.

There has undoubtedly been a shift in emphasis during this century away from the hope of heaven to a hope of making this earth a better place. This is no bad thing. Indeed, insofar as the hope of heaven distracted people from doing something about this world's ills, it is a positive good. There is also no doubt that previous generations sometimes had a much more pessimistic view about life on earth than people do today. Today we want to affirm all that is good in this life, and above all the experience of living within it. But this does not mean to say we should or can afford to sit light to the hope of the fulfilment of God's Kingdom. On the contrary, hope that God's justice will ultimately prevail, that, as Paul put it, in the end God will be all in all, is an essential feature of Christian belief. It is true that a surprisingly large number of church people seem to regard it as an optional extra. It is true that a good number of Jews, whilst affirming the goodness of God and this life which he has created, do not believe there is any other. Nevertheless my own view is that it is one of the pillars of belief without which the whole building is likely to come tumbling down.

Winston Churchill, when asked whether there was a life after death, replied that there may very well be two worlds but he preferred to take them one at a time. So may we. Indeed we have been set on this earth to live life to the full, and to do what we can to make existence here reflect more adequately God's purpose for it. But hope is essential, hope that God's justice will finally prevail, that, in the end, as T.S. Eliot put it in *Four Quartets* quoting Julian of Norwich:

> And all shall be well
> And all manner of thing shall be well.

This is not an optional extra but a central conviction of Christian belief. We do not need even to attempt to describe how this hope may be realized. All we need do is aspire to die as Luke records Jesus dying, with the words 'Father, into thy hands I commend my Spirit', in trust that God is faithful and in hope that his purpose towards us and the world as a whole will find its proper fulfilment.

Chapter 8

CANCER AND THE
MUSIC OF GOD

In chapter two of this book I suggested that religious faith was in
a profound and proper sense 'natural'. This does not mean that I
take the arguments against the validity of belief lightly. On the
contrary, I take them with the utmost seriousness. But it means
that the main weight of the argument against God falls on the
existence of so much evil and suffering in the world. It is
natural, on my view, to believe that there is a wise and loving
God – but the longer we live, the more aware we become of the
extent of human anguish. As we can come to mistrust someone
we at first believed in, so we can come to lose all faith in a
trustworthy God. The cruelty and suffering that abounds keeps
pushing us in that direction. Something therefore must be said
about this, if faith is to be retained at all. Furthermore it is also
necessary to take up the problem raised in the first chapter, of
how God works in the world. If God does not 'intervene', so far
as we know, to stop the assassination of John Kennedy or the
attempted assassination of the Pope, what does he do, if
anything? And if he does nothing, how is this to be distinguished
from there being no real God at all, which is Freeman's view?

First, an obvious point. Much suffering in the world is caused
by the negligence, weakness and deliberate wrongdoing of
human beings. If it is the will of God to create free beings, as
opposed to robots or puppets, this is the price he and we have to
pay. It is true that some philosophers have suggested that God
could have created us free, in such a way that we would always
freely choose to do right. On this view God would be like a
hypnotist who tells us under hypnosis how we should act. We
would think we were deciding things for ourselves but in fact we
would have been programmed by God. It would have been quite
possible to create a universe in which this happened. But there is

one fatal flaw. God himself would know he had cheated. He, at least, would know that we were not acting with genuine freedom but only in response to suggestions given us under hypnosis.

If we value being able to make up our own minds and make our own decisions in life then we too have to pay the price of living in a world in which this is possible. We cannot have it both ways. We cannot both be free to make choices and have a world in which wrong choices do no damage. This point, if accepted, has wide implications for much more suffering in the world is attributable to human beings than we sometimes allow. Take the millions of starving people. The fact is that there is quite enough food in the world for everyone. But through millions of wrong choices which have brought about the rigid political and economic structures in which we live, there are mountains of surplus food in Europe and America, whilst those in Africa starve to death.

So a great deal of suffering in the world is caused by human beings. But not all of it. There is disease. There are natural disasters. Two points can be made about this. First, God does not simply make the world. He does something much more sophisticated. He makes the world make itself. He gives everything in the universe, from the subatomic particles of which matter is composed, through electrons, atoms, cells, up to multi-cellular structures like ourselves, a life of its own. In fact, when we think about it, a life of our own is the only kind of life we could have. If we did not have a life of our own we would not exist at all and this is true of the atom and the amoeba as much as of us. God has given the basic elements of matter a life of their own and has woven the universe from the bottom upwards through the free interplay of millions of forces. In all this interplay what we call accidents occur the whole time. But accidents are not in themselves harmful. For example, think of volcanoes and earthquakes. These occur because the plant called 'Earth', on which we live, has reached a particular stage in its cooling. This is also the stage which made it possible for life to emerge. If the earth was still molten there would be no life. If it had cooled to become a solid cold ball there would be no life. It has in fact cooled enough to allow a crust to form, on which life has been able to develop. But because it is a crust and not a solid ball the inner plates of the earth are still free to slide about a little, and the molten material inside the earth can on occasion find a way out of the crust. There is nothing wrong with these movements and eruptions in themselves. They are just examples of the millions and millions of clashes and combinations that occur every second at every level of the universe. They are not essentially different from the billowing of clouds or the movements of water in a stream.

The second point is that in order to exist as the kind of creatures we are, capable of thinking and choosing, we need a relatively stable environment. I plan my day and make decisions about it on the basis of certain well-founded assumptions: the sun will come up, the laws of gravity will operate, water will boil at a certain temperature and freeze at another one. The consequences of what I do, putting on the electric kettle or putting water in the freezer, are predictable. This means that there is a very strict limit on what God can do in the way of disrupting these scientific laws without frustrating his whole purpose in making the universe in the first place. It might be amusing to live in an Alice in Wonderland type of world but our amusement would only last a few seconds. If we suddenly started to shrink in an uncontrollable way or float up to the ceiling we literally would not know whether we were coming or going. If we were born into that kind of environment we would never learn to think at all. For thinking necessitates continuity between one day's experience and the next. If a child went to school and was told that the sign A symbolized an A sound and the next day was told that the same sign really indicated a B sound, that child would never learn to read, for learning involves building on present experience in a predictable way. So it is with our environment as a whole. Sometimes we long for God to 'intervene' to stop some terrible accident in a miraculous way, but where would it stop? Suppose you are driving along and a young child runs out in front of the car. Normally you would hit the child but a miracle occurs and you pull up short in ten feet instead of the expected 30 feet. That would be wonderful. But what about the car just behind you? In order to prevent that car bumping into you, another miracle would have to occur. And what about the car behind that one? In other words a single alteration to the laws of nature (which are only laws in the sense that they are observed regularities on the basis of which we can make predictions) would have ramifications throughout the universe. And would it be fair to limit the miracle to one tiny point? If a miracle was performed to enable the first car to pull up in a few feet but not the second one, the driver of the second one could very well claim that it was unjust, for he had been driving along at the correct speed allowing for a proper stopping distance at that speed. He had not taken into account that a miracle would occur just in front of him – and why should he?

This is not in any way to deny that God works in his universe. According to Christian belief he is at the very heart of things, closer to us than our own breathing. Furthermore he works out his purpose through us, particularly when we co-operate with him in prayer. Indeed prayer itself may allow God to work through us in his universe in mysterious ways that we are not fully aware of. Nor is it to deny that full-blooded miracles, in the sense of a suspension of the laws of nature, may sometimes occur. The point is that there is a very severe limit to what God can do in this way without spoiling what it is all about – namely bringing into existence creatures like you and me, who are capable of thinking for ourselves and making real choices. For in order to exist as the kind of people we are, we need an environment characterized by continuity, stability, regularity and predictability.

The question arises, however, why God made us part of a material world. Much suffering arises from the fact that we are vulnerable creatures of flesh and blood, set in an environment which often seems very hard, as when a river floods and drowns many people. Why did not God simply create us as free spiritual beings like angels? No one really knows the answer to that question except God. All we can do is guess. The best guess comes from Austin Farrer. He argued that God bound us up with a physical universe in order to preserve our freedom to respond to him or not. We would be drawn by his incandescent beauty and holiness like moths to a candle or metal filings to a magnet. So in order that we might have real freedom of manoeuvre, God puts us at a distance from himself – not a physical distance, because that is impossible as God is closer to us than we are to ourselves, but a distance of knowing. He made us physical beings in a physical world which can act as a kind of veil between us and himself. The result is that on this earth we have no immediate and overwhelming knowledge of God. Further-more we are born with a strong drive to preserve our life in being. We only come to a knowledge of God at all in so far as we are capable of growing out of our self-centredness and are willing to live before one who, by definition, makes a total difference to our lives. The knowledge of God is rarely overwhelming and inescapable. For most people there is only a flickering, dawning awareness which is always related to our willingness to know and love God. In this way God preserves our freedom and ensures that the pilgrimage we make is our own journey. (This guess has two implications, both of which I accept. First, angels are not as free as human beings. They are totally transparent to the bidding of God. Second, there was no fall of angels, for they were created perfect in the immediate presence of God.) We, however, have not been created perfect. We have instead been created with the possibility of achieving perfection of a different (and higher) kind than the angels. And we have not been created in the immediate presence of God. We have been made in such a way that we have to make our journey towards him.

So God has created a physical universe, which makes itself from the bottom upwards in ever more complex forms of life, until *we* emerge, as part of that physical universe, yet with the possibility of developing as rational, moral and spiritual beings; half ape, half angel, as Disraeli put it. This physical universe is characterized by reliability and predictability. We are now, for example, beginning to be able to predict hurricanes, earthquakes and volcanoes, and to take steps to avert their worst effects on us.

But what, we might say, is God doing in all this? First, God is holding the whole universe in being and enabling each tiny constituent part of it to go on being itself. We tend to take this for granted. But why should each electron, atom and cell of the universe both be there and go on retaining its essential characteristics in such a way that it can combine to make higher forms of life? Religious believers claim this is so only because God, the source and fount of all being, holds everything in existence and does so in a way that reflects his own constancy. For the laws of nature, which we think of as so hard and impersonal, almost as an iron necessity, in fact reflect God's undeviating constancy and faithfulness. When the steam arises from a boiling kettle, or rain drops fall from the sky or a breeze dries the washing, these are expressions of the faithfulness of God, his steady constancy, his utter reliability.

Second, God himself feels the anguish of the universe. It is of the very nature of love to enter imaginatively into the situation of others and, to some extent, feel what they feel. God who is perfect love knows every point of the universe from the inside and bears it within his heart. The word sympathy comes from two Greek words meaning 'to suffer with'. God suffers with his creation. When Jesus was tortured to death this was an expression, in human terms, of the pain God bears eternally.

Third, God is ceaselessly at work bringing good out of evil. When a tragedy occurs he inspires first sympathy and then practical action. He never stops in his work of making accident and disaster yield some good.

Fourth, the purpose of God cannot finally be defeated. Christ died a terrible death on the cross apparently feeling that God had abandoned him: 'My God, my God, why has thou forsaken me?' But God raised him from the dead to live for ever in a new kind of way altogether, as an ever present spiritual presence. The purpose of love cannot finally be defeated.

Fifth, God has promised us an eternal existence with himself. He knows each one of us through and through and he will re-create our real self in a form appropriate to an eternal existence. Heaven lies ahead for those who will appreciate it.

The case against the idea that there is a God of love behind the universe is very strong. Indeed so strong that it is only on the basis of these five points, taken together, that it is possible to hold such a belief. Belief in eternity can hardly be an optional extra, for example, when so many people die young with their potential unrealized. If there is no further state beyond this life for them to develop in, how can we believe there is a God of love? Similarly if Christ was not raised from the dead, how can we believe either in him or the God in whom he trusted? For he trusted his heavenly Father to the bitter end, even through the darkness of despair. It is only on the basis of these five points that we can believe that love made the world. But these five points are also the evidence *for* the love of God. They provide not only the case for the defence but evidence for positive belief.

The evidence that there is a God of love is based on our belief that the world has a genuine independence. We are not a dream of God or simply an expression of his body. His love is so great that he has made a world with a life of its own and brought to the light of consciousness creatures who even have the power to frustrate his purpose. But this is not an indifferent, impassive God. God bears our travail and anguish within himself. So much so that he has come amongst us and experienced as a human person the worst that life can do. Yet this is not a God who was irresponsible enough to make a world over which he would lose all control. Making the world was a huge risk but it was a risk he took in the confidence he could bring it to its natural fulfilment. Of this the resurrection of Christ is the expression and pledge. God's love cannot be defeated. He raised Christ from the dead and he will re-create each one of us anew for an eternal existence. As a father gives his children good gifts, so God will share with us his own immortality made manifest in Christ. This is very powerful evidence for the love of God. Believing in a God of love does not mean that horrible things do not happen. They do happen, all the time, for the reasons outlined earlier. The evidence for a God of love comes from a different source, from the five points just stated.

Although it is possible to understand some of the reasons why, if God was going to make creatures like us, the world has to have more or less the character of the world we know, it is still possible to wonder whether it is all worth it. A child's cry: 'Don't kill me, mum.' makes us ask if God was really justified in creating a world in which he knew such things would happen? For even if there is an eternity ahead of that murdered child, nothing can change the fact that he was killed by his own mother and that he knew what was happening to him. This is the question of Ivan, one of the brothers in Dostoyevsky's novel *The Brothers Karamazov*. After recounting various stories of cruelty to children he asked if God was justified in making such a world. He then went on to argue that whatever harmony might be achieved in some heavenly future, nothing could justify such cruelty to children on the way. It wasn't that he disbelieved in God, he said. He just wanted to return his ticket.

This is a powerful point, yet at least three things can be said which put a somewhat different perspective on the matter. First,

the question of whether life is worth it or not is a question each
one of us has to answer for himself. No one can reply for us and
we cannot presume to answer for others, however ghastly their
circumstances seem to us. For when we come across someone in
hospital, perhaps paralysed from the neck downwards, our
instinctive reaction is that we could not bear to live life under
such conditions. We would rather be dead. Yet often such people
show extraordinary courage and even cheerfulness, enhancing
life for others in a most moving way. Whether, despite
everything, life is worth living is a question only they can
answer. Second, the courage and endurance which so many show
in life seems to witness to the fact that something desperately
important is at stake in human life, and it is not simply a matter
of weighing up the pleasure against the pain. If it was simply a
matter of weighing up the pleasure against the pain, far more
people would commit suicide. But the vast majority of people do
not commit suicide. They go struggling on with humour and
fortitude, their lives, as someone once said, like flowers growing
in a bed of concrete. In D.H. Lawrence's novel *Sons and Lovers*,
Paul Morel visits his mother, who is dying of cancer, and she
chides him because his life is all struggle. She says she wants
him to be happy. But Paul says that there is something more
important than happiness and unhappiness: he wants to live. By
that he did not mean live it up. He wanted to live with all the
courage and creativity within him.

Third, there are sometimes experiences in human life when a
glorious goal makes the difficult journey to it seem worthwhile,
as when a runner after years of hard training wins a gold medal
at the Olympic Games. Or there are times when a glorious
experience can make the pain of the past drop away, as when an
engaged couple who have been separated for a year and only
able to communicate by 'phone and letter come together again.
All the pain of missing one another and the inevitable
misunderstandings suddenly fade into the background.

If at the end of the whole creative process, beyond space and
time when, as St Paul put it, God is all in all, everyone who has
ever lived is able to bless God for their existence, then the
unbiased critic must admit that God was justified in taking the
risk of creating a universe. For all who have gone through the
experience will say for themselves: 'Praise the Lord O my soul,

all that is within me, praise his holy name.' This would be heaven. Of course suffering will not be totally forgotten. In the stories of Christ's appearance to his disciples, the wounds remain. But they are healed and transfigured, taken into a new, deeper reality in which they too have a part to play. This vision of an ultimate state of affairs in which all is well is a hope. But it is a hope that is witnessed to not only by the Christian faith but by the practical example of countless millions of people, of all faiths and none, who live lives with great courage. For they seem to have an intuitive sense that something vastly important is at stake in all this human travail. In old-fashioned language, what is at stake is the making of our eternal souls.

On Karl Marx's grave in Highgate cemetery are carved his famous words 'Philosophers have only interpreted the world, the point is, however, to change it'. Christians have much sympathy with that statement. For they do not offer a philosophical answer to the problem of suffering, as though it were something to be resigned to. They offer a vision of an ultimate state of affairs in which suffering as we know it no longer exists, a state of affairs which has to be worked for. It is true that the new heaven and earth of which the Bible speaks go beyond our space and time but they have to be reached for and built up on this earth. The answer to the problem of suffering is not an idea or a theology but an actual state of affairs, which does not yet exist, but which offers us a vision of what, under God, can come about if we co-operate with God in his work. There are some very important practical implications of this.

First, suffering is contrary to the will of God. In the gospels Jesus is shown healing the physically and mentally sick, casting out demons, calling sinners to change their ways. His ministry is an invasion of the forces of goodness and light against all that blights and hurts human life. There may be a sense in which God is responsible for everything, in that he created the universe. But a sharp distinction has to be made between what God directly wills and what he merely permits as part of his overall purpose. So a parent may be responsible for giving his child permission to drive the family car. But he in no sense wills the subsequent accident that unfortunately occurs. God wills the universe to exist, he lets it be with a life of its own. But he does not will suffering; on the contrary, he opposes it. Christ, the image of

God, brings life and health. So Christians, following his example, have founded hospitals, leper colonies, hospices and all manner of institutions dedicated to relieving the sick.

Second, God is ceaselessly at work bringing good out of evil and we are called to co-operate with him in this task. For it is the particular work of God not only to oppose all that mars human life but to make what mars our lives yield some good fruit. So sickness can bring about sympathy and practical support from friends and a deeper understanding of life from the sufferer. Here we have to be very careful. Whilst it is true that many good qualities and actions can come out of sickness or tragedy, God does not design horrible situations in order to bring this good out of them. Such a God would be intolerable. If a friend tripped us up on the stairs and broke our leg in order to see whether we would develop qualities of patience and endurance under adversity we would not think much of his or her friendship: indeed we would not call him or her a friend. So with God. God, like a good friend, wants things to go well with us. He is not about to pull the carpet from under us to see how we we react. For good breeds more good than evil can. A comfortable home, with enough to eat, caring parents and an interest in sport or culture is much more likely to give children a chance to develop as healthy personalities than a home that is impoverished or stricken in one way or another. The parents in such a home may be very caring but if they are continually worried about money, have little time to give to their children because they have to work so hard, if they live in poor physical surroundings or are stricken with mental illness, then the children are likely to be affected. Good breeds more good than evil can. It is the particular mercy of God to make even evil yield some good.

Everyone knows someone who under adversity has developed admirable qualities. We have all been involved in tragic or difficult situations which have brought the best out of people. This is all summed up in some lines of the poet Edwin Muir. He contrasts our sad world with the apparently perfect conditions of the Garden of Eden, but concludes:

> But famished field and blackened tree
> Bear flowers in Eden never known;
> Blossoms of grief and charity

Bloom in these darkened fields alone.
What had Eden ever to say
Of hope and faith and pity and love . . .
Strange blessings never in Paradise
Fall from these beclouded skies.[24]

There is a tightrope to walk here. God does not will suffering.
On the contrary he wills us to relieve and eliminate it, so far as
we can. Yet out of suffering can come hope and faith and pity
and love. God did not design the beclouded skies in order that
the strange blessings might fall from them. Yet fall they do,
making life look very different. The weighing of goods and evils
is notoriously difficult and should not be done. A husband who
has just lost a dearly loved wife does not want to be told that he
has become a much deeper, more understanding person as a
result. He would rather have his wife back. A man whose son
has been killed in a motor-bike accident may spend the rest of
his life helping youth clubs and do much good work. But he
would rather have his son back. Yet if there is an eternal destiny,
the good which people see coming out of evil will one day find
its proper place. For if we have been made to grow more and
more like God, so that we can live with him in the communion
of saints, the deepening of a person in a bereavement or the good
work that people undertake as a result of a tragedy, are
considerations of ultimate significance.

The thoughts put forward here are only of very limited use,
and no use at all when a person is in anguish. When a person is
afflicted with physical or mental pain they want understanding
and practical help. They do not want religious consolation or
attempts to 'justify the ways of God to men'. Nevertheless, there
is a limited use for the kind of considerations adduced here on
other occasions. For, as has been admitted, the case against the
idea that love made the world is a formidable one. Unless
something sensible is said, faith can ebb away and hope die.
There is no intellectual solution to the problem of suffering and
certainly no knock-down arguments. All that is possible is to say
enough to go on living in faith and hope and love. For,
paradoxically, the very strength of the case against the notion of
a God of love reveals more clearly the evidence *for* a God of
love. This evidence, as considered earlier, has five features.

First, God has given us a real independence. He has *created* us rather than dreamt us. Second, God himself feels our anguish with us. Third, he is ceaselessly at work forcing even evil to yield some good. Fourth, as the resurrection of Christ reveals, his purpose cannot finally be defeated. And fifth, God has promised us an eternal existence, if we are ready to receive it. A character in a novel by Rebecca West says at one point: 'What's the good of music if there's all this cancer in the world?' To this someone else responds: 'What's the harm of cancer, if there's all this music in the world?' Music can lift people into a dimension in which life seems very different. This is even more true of the love of God. A knowledge of the love of God does not stop tragedy being tragedy or suffering suffering. There is no glossing over, no pretending that all is for the best. For manifestly all is not for the best; a great deal is for the worst. But the love of God, of which we all have some practical proof in the sheer existence of our own being, but which is definitively disclosed in the life, death and resurrection of Christ together with the promises to us inherent in Christ, is a kind of music which makes us see, in our best moments, what really matters and what does not matter quite so much.

There is no purely intellectual solution. Instead the Christian faith offers a vision of what the love of God is in the course of achieving. We are called to co-operate with that love by relieving suffering, eliminating its causes in poverty and disease and by responding to things going wrong in as constructive and positive a way as possible. For so it is that God's purpose is furthered. A sense of how much suffering there is in life can lead us either to deny our maker or to care for his world. The more we care, the more conscious we will be of the affliction which besets us. But the more we care the more certain we will be that the world which is afflicted is good. And in caring we will be at one with the caring of God.

CHAPTER 9

REASONS FOR ENCHANTMENT

The reason why some people believe and others do not is a mystery. No doubt a number of factors are involved. What seems clear is that faith gets into a person before they are aware of it. I can remember at school a friend of mine suddenly saying that there was no God. Instinctively I found myself blurting out that there was. But, so far as I know, I had never given the matter a moment's thought. I had had little in the way of religious upbringing. What went on in school chapel did not interest me. Did I blurt out that there was a God simply because I had been indoctrinated and was fairly conventional? Or was it a case of 'out of the mouths of babes and sucklings'? In any case, something, somewhere along the line had gone in and taken hold, perhaps with my mother's milk. For in due course the seed that was there grew.

At the end of her novel *The Towers of Trebizond*, Rose Macaulay describes how certain facts in her life kept her outside full membership of the Church, but how the Christian faith, pictured as a kind of city, still held her:

> Still the Towers of Trebizond, the fabled city, shimmer on a far horizon, gated and walled and held in a luminous enchantment. It seems that for me, however much I must stand outside them, this must for ever be.[25]

The vision of a world created by a good God, a God who comes amongst us to share our life, a God who brings us to share his own immortality with all the company of the faithful, is in the end a kind of luminous enchantment. It arises in response to the marvel and beauty of the world, as the mind moves to the one whom Augustine addressed in the words: 'O thou beauty most ancient and with all so fresh'. It arises in response to the beauty of certain lives, either met personally or read about, the beauty of holiness, which has its source in the holiness of God himself. It arises in response to the beauty, however simple, of certain acts of worship or forms of prayer. It arises in response to depictions of the world from a Christian point of view in great works of art, novels, music, poetry, drama. It arises when misconceptions are stripped away and we can see the world from a Christian point of view, even taking evil fully into account, as I tried to do in the previous chapter.

In Evelyn Waugh's novel *Brideshead Revisited*, Charles Ryder queried his friend's beliefs:

> 'But my dear Sebastian, you can't *seriously* believe.'
> 'Can't I?'
> 'I mean about Christmas and the star and the
>   three kings and the ox and the ass.'
> 'Oh yes, I believe that. It's a lovely idea.'
> 'But you can't *believe* things because they're
>   a lovely idea.'
> 'But I *do*. That's how I believe.'[26]

What I have written above indicates some sympathy with Sebastian's point of view. It is the sheer loveliness of the Christian understanding of God, which can come across for example in the Christmas story, which attracts us and holds us. Yet, like Charles Ryder, we want to assert that we can't believe things just because they are a lovely idea. We want to say that the Christian faith is a rational belief, a belief that rational beings can hold, and not just a fairy story.

What constitutes a rational belief and what counts as evidence to justify it is not quite the same across the board. It will not be just the same for a historian or a physicist, a sociologist or mathematician. What I mean by a rational belief in religion is one that can do justice to the character of the world as a whole and make sense of it in its entirety; it helps things fall into place and discloses the meaning even of suffering.

A belief in a God who is the source of all that is, makes sense of why anything is here at all. A belief that this God is good and wills to make us in his own image, makes sense of why he should have toiled through millions and millions of years of evolution to bring creation to a focus in each one of us. A belief that there is a rational intelligence behind the universe, makes sense of the fact that the world discloses its secrets to patient scientific discovery. For scientists are more and more struck how the universe yields patterns that combine complexity and simplicity, symmetry and beauty, which can be expressed in mathematical formulae and scientific equations. A belief that behind life there is a holy God who calls us to holiness, makes sense of the strong sense of duty many people have and the conscience we all share, even those who are not particularly religious.

None of this is proof. Proof is not possible from either a philosophical or theological standpoint. Proofs (and disproofs) always leave the matter open. Nevertheless there is evidence for those with eyes to see: the existence of the universe itself in all its wondrous complexity and beauty; evidence in myself, in my capacity to think and choose and love; evidence in the sheer goodness of some people's lives; evidence in the pattern and form that runs through everything, from a leaf to a galaxy. How we interpret this evidence will depend in significant measure on our background beliefs and assumptions. This is the case with all interpretation of evidence, whether in science or history. For example, most of us look for a natural explanation of the circles which appear in fields of wheat in summer. We are disinclined to attribute such phenomena to visitors from another planet, because we do not believe in such visitors. Because we believe in the power of scientific explanation for so many matters, we look to it to explain these circles as well. But we do not come to the evidence as totally neutral observers. We come with certain assumptions about scientific or natural explanation.

If we pray for someone who is ill and, much to everyone's surprise, they recover, our natural tendency as people shaped by the twentieth century, will be to attribute a natural explanation to this also. But if we believe that God is real, that God has our well-being at heart, that his spirit is ceaselessly at work in our lives, especially in and through our prayers, then we will not rule out another explanation. An atheist of course would not even consider this alternative. But for someone who believes in the

God disclosed to us in the Bible, it will always be a possibility. People's beliefs and assumptions can be totally misguided. But we always bring them to bear in interpreting evidence. This means that some evidence, against some background beliefs, can appear compelling to one observer, whilst others remain unconvinced.

One way in which the Christian faith is a live option for rational beings is that, in its light, everything falls most wonderfully into place. Even the terrible evil and suffering of the world can bring out the depths of divine love in the way suggested in the previous chapter. There is however one important qualification. For me this comes to a head in the doctrine of karma, the belief that we are working out in this life the good and ill effects of the way we acted in previous lives. This has the corollary that how we act now will determine the state we find ourselves in in future existences. This has always seemed to me a wonderfully neat doctrine; it seems so logical and fair. Everyone in the end gets their just deserts, in a way that is strict and inevitable. I find difficulty in believing it on philosophical grounds because of the question of personal identity. In what way could the self that I am now possibly have been a Chinese peasant or a Roman slave? But more to the point for present purposes, it fails to catch the tragic quality of human existence. Life as we know it has an inescapable tragic dimension, the good really does get defeated by evil. This very often has the effect of revealing the goodness of the good even more clearly, but nevertheless it does not always seem to win. The Christian faith does capture this tragic sense and make room for it, as focused in the cross of Christ. Even though we believe, through the resurrection of Jesus, a pledge of God's final triumph over evil, that life is not ultimately tragic, nevertheless we must recognize and acknowledge the tragic dimension for what it is. So far as I have seen, this is absent from a Hindu view. So when I say that the Christian faith makes sense of life in its entirety, I include that sense of the tragic, which is why in the end a Christian approach to the problem of suffering seems to do more justice to the actual quality of existence than the doctrine of karma. This leads on to an even more fundamental point. What constitutes rational justification of belief varies from one culture to another.

One of the most widely shared assumptions of modern thought is that we have no absolute standpoint from which to judge rival claims to the truth. We are bedded down in a particular culture, at a particular time in history and the tradition in which we find ourselves will have its own developed standards of rational justification. We have no bird's eye view above all traditions of critical enquiry.

The implications of this for moral philosophy have been worked out in a thorough-going way by Alisdair MacIntyre.[27] He believes that all our concepts of right and wrong are related to the roles and responsibilities exercised by particular people in particular cultures. We should not try to detach the notion of 'duty', for example, from the culture in which it was clearly defined in relation to generally accepted norms of conduct associated with particular public offices or roles. Since the eighteenth century Enlightenment however, this attempt to detach moral concepts from the cultures in which they have been used, is just what moral philosophy has tried to achieve. It has tried to discover universally acceptable ways of defining duty, right, wrong, the good etc. But this cannot be done and has led moral philosophy to its present impasse. For moral concepts cannot be divorced from our whole understanding of human nature, which varies from tradition to tradition, and which is integrally related to particular philosophical and religious notions about what human beings really are. Furthermore western philosophical liberalism, which has tried to discover rational ways of straddling all traditions of enquiry, is itself a tradition. It is not an absolute vantage point above all traditions. It too is a product of history and has a history.

Does this mean then that we are all doomed to a permanent relativism? To thinking that each society, or each tradition within society, will have its own standards of what constitutes the truth, which can never engage or be settled? MacIntyre resolutely refuses to draw this conclusion.

He argues, rightly in my view, that because each tradition is committed to the truth of its claims, it is thereby also committed to examining the claims of rival traditions. In order to do this, it has to formulate those claims, and in order to formulate them, it has to translate them into the terms of its own tradition. This means that rival traditions will inevitably be brought together with comparable standards of rational justification. Even if one tradition comes to the conclusion that there is no real meeting, that the claims are incommensurable, this judgement of itself assumes that there has been some genuine contact, some common ground. Conversely, if those other traditions reject our own, to do this they will have to have some understanding of what it is doing, and this will have involved an act of translation into terms which they could recognize and argue with.

Any tradition committed to the truth of its own point of view must at the same time be committed to a dialectical relationship with rival traditions, in which conversation takes place, conversation which will inevitably involve some shared understanding of what might count for and against the truth of the claims in question.

The principles and assumptions that MacIntyre brings to bear on moral philosophy are also appropriate to religious claims. To be sure, the problems associated with adjudicating between different religious claims loom even larger than they do between different moral claims. It seems easier to discover ways in common of talking about right and wrong, for we all have to live in society, whether we are religious or not. But the difference in difficulty is not so large as might first be thought, because as MacIntyre shows, moral concepts have been integrally related to particular understandings of human nature, and these have involved philosophical and religious perspectives about the end or goal of human existence.

The different claims of different religions constitute a real problem which cannot be glossed over by any simplistic talk that of course all religions are really saying the same thing. They are not. Sometimes they offer alternative, mutually exclusive, ways of viewing the world. This can make it very difficult for one religion truly to understand another. One person who is highly aware of this is the Japanese novelist Shusako Endo. Himself a Roman Catholic, he knows how difficult it is for those imbued with Japanese culture to grasp the distinctive nature of Christianity. For example, both western culture and Japanese culture may be aware of the passingness of all things, of our mortality. But it can seem that Japanese culture relishes the evanescence, the fleetingness of things. It savours the poignancy. The result is that one of the images in Endo's novels is the swamp. Everything, including the most distinctive beliefs of Christian faith, is pulled into a swamp where one thing can hardly be distinguished from another.

This would seem to undermine MacIntyre's point. For it suggests that the process of understanding another point of view in terms of one's own, will inevitably drain that other point of view of its distinctiveness. And clearly there is always that danger. But what the Christian, or any other adherent of the rival tradition would have to do, is to continue the dialogue, to say that the Japanese in question have not yet understood what Christianity is, or what they mean by mortality and finitude. The dialogue must go on until all the partners to it are confident that their point of view, their understanding of the truth and how it is to be justified, has been understood in its own terms. I have deliberately chosen an extreme example. Other religious traditions are much closer to one another than Christianity and a traditional Japanese religion. They can more easily come to a common understanding, not about what truth in its final form might consist of, but about how such truth might be recognized or justified.

Three principles emerge from this. Any religion, like Christianity, that claims to be true, need not give up that claim just because there are rival claimants to the truth, with apparently different standards of what constitutes rational justification for it. Second, however, just because it claims to be the truth, a truth that can be recognized by rational beings, it is thereby committed to dialogue with rival ways of seeing and arguing. Third, this dialogue will be a continuing one, with no foreseeable end this side of kingdom come.

This leads to a further point. We can only know the true meaning of something when we see it as part of the whole of which it is part. With history, this means that we can only know the true significance of an event when we have the whole sweep of history before us, and that means in the light of its end point. For every event is subject to continual reinterpretation. Historians, for example, are constantly re-examining the causes of World War II and each generation will have a slightly different emphasis, as it sees those events in a wider perspective, from a longer view, or in the light of newly discovered facts. The true story can only be told at the end, when all can be seen in its place, as part of the whole. It is not at all surprising, therefore, that all through the Hebrew Scriptures people are looking to the future, to the time when God's Kingdom will be established, or that in the New Testament Christians do the same. It is in the light shed by the end of time, that all will be made clear. Christians believe that in the life, death and resurrection of Jesus the end has already drawn near, and we live in the faith that in Christ evil and death have in principle been overcome and that there can be life with God for ever, beginning now. We know this in a fragmentary, anticipatory way for ourselves. We do not yet know it for creation as a whole. St Paul wrote:

> For now we see in a mirror dimly, but then face to face. Now I know in part; then I shall understand fully, even as I have been fully understood. (1 Corinthians 13.12)

For a Christian then, standards of rational justification will be illumined by Christ. Our understanding of human fulfilment, for example, will not be the same as a secular one. There will be overlap, but in the end it will be defined by growing into 'the full stature of Christ'. Nevertheless although there are standards which are particular to our tradition, just because we claim that that tradition yields the truth, we are thereby committed to a serious and honest dialogue with rival traditions. My own experience is that such dialogue is mutually enriching and enlarging. We receive and we give. In this dialogue rival traditions of the truth, and of how the truth is to be established or justified, come together in a way which reveals common ground and a journey to the fullness of truth on the basis of a map that both can read. There will still be deep disagreements about how to get there and indeed about where it is that we are trying to reach, but both can begin to understand the same map – and that is the only point, a fundamental one, which is being made here. Standards of rational justification, though arising within each tradition, are not incommensurable.

It is fashionable today to stress the contrast between different periods in history and different cultures. But the continuity and similarities are no less striking. There is, for example, much more agreement on fundamental moral norms than is often recognized. When there is disagreement, there is often an appeal to a standard which both partners to the discussion accept. Indeed there is nothing very odd about the extent of this agreement. Given the fact that we all share the same basic biochemical make-up, we have all evolved together and we all have to live and survive in human society, this is just what we would expect. What is true of moral standards has a bearing on what we consider as counting for or against the truth of things. In order to highlight the problem and indicate that there is a way forward I will take some recent discussion on the biblical figure of Hagar. Because Abraham and Sarah seemed unable to have a child Sarah gave her handmaid, Hagar, to her husband. Hagar conceived but her pride in maternity so incensed Sarah that she was ill-treated and thrown out. In the desert she encountered God and was told to go back to her mistress (Genesis chapters 16 and 21).

The biblical narrative in Genesis is primarily interested in the people of Israel and God's assurance of their future through the miraculous birth of Isaac to Abraham and Sarah in their old age. Hagar and her son Ishmael are marginal. Hagar is an oppressed figure, subservient to the main thrust of the story as she was to her master and mistress.

Feminist biblical scholarship has been concerned to recover the figure of Hagar. Any sensitive person reading the Bible will sometimes have wondered about the unfair, cruel treatment of Hagar and others like her in the Scriptures. Feminist criticism builds on this feeling in order to rescue Hagar as a real figure, an oppressed woman who, against all the odds, tries to stand up for herself. Yet feminist theology has in its turn been accused by black women theologians of being 'white and racist'. This is because it assumes a universal women's experience, when in fact this is nothing more than the experience of white, middle-class women. This is very different from say the experience of black working-class women and an awareness of difference, leading to dialogue, should be the starting-point of true theology.

Recently these different points of view have been brought together in an interesting article by Kathy Taylor.[28] She takes Celie from Alice Walker's novel *The Color Purple* and sets her beside Hagar in a series of contrasts. One big difference is that Celie in the novel is able to speak for herself whereas Hagar is the subject of a narrative that oppresses and marginalizes her.

Celie, through standing up for herself, achieves a degree of
liberation from oppression. Hagar can only point to the
possibility of a liberation that she did not achieve. What we have
here is the beginning of a dialogue or conversation between
people with very different starting-points: the narrator of
Genesis whose over-whelming concern is the future of the
people of Israel; white feminist biblical scholars who rescue
Hagar as a woman; black feminist scholars who rescue Hagar as
a black, oppressed woman. The author brings people with these
stand-points into the same circle. What is important, from the
stand-point of this book, is that people with very different
perspectives *can* come together, not on the basis of some
allegedly universal, but in fact partial and imposed, point of
view but from their very different starting-points. And, at the
same time, running through the dialogue are some commonly
accepted notions, notions in which the moral and the
metaphysical are integrally bound together; for example, that
liberation from oppression is a worthwhile goal. The Old
Testament narrative applies it primarily to the deliverance of
Israel from Egypt, but this is widened out and applied by the
other participants to non-Jews (Hagar was an Egyptian), to
women, to black people, to slaves. There is a developing
assumption that people ought to be able to speak for themselves
and stand up for themselves, even before God, against all forms
of oppression.

The dialogue or conversation that has begun here could be
widened. As it stands, it mainly involves people shaped by the
Judaeo-Christian tradition. There would be a bigger challenge,
for example, in bringing in a Japanese Buddhist. But, as Alastair
MacIntyre has so rightly argued, a commitment to truth demands
that the circle be continually widened to include those whose
starting-points may be very different from those already in the
circle.

The starting-point of the narrative in Genesis is a good God
who creates us in his own image and wants our well-being. In
the modern world we cannot assume that 'well-being' means
exactly the same to different people. There is common ground.
Christians and atheists, like good parents, will agree that people
ought to be able to develop all the talent and potential they have
within them. This means creating the right material conditions

and educational environment for them. But there is also divergence. For a Christian, well-being means growth in spiritual qualities, in love and joy and peace, in the knowledge of God and care for other people. In evaluating whether the world makes sense, whether things fall into place, we bear in mind that the goal is eternal life. Existence, on a Christian view, cannot be seen in terms of a calculus of pain and pleasure. It is about physical, mental and emotional growth, together with spiritual growth that can continue even during the years of physical decline. This means that Hagar and the millions and millions like her who have led subjugated, suffering lives have hope. This sounds incredible, impossible to believe. But there is a logic of love as well as a logic of the mind: and the logic of divine love points to the fulfilment of all those made in the divine image, even when this takes us beyond the limits set by space and time. The implication is that if we are exploring the rationality of belief, we cannot do this in isolation from our whole understanding of what is being achieved and what is at stake.

Our awareness of living in a multi-cultural world, far from leading to relativism and despair about the possibility of objective truth, should lead to a greater confidence that the truth can in fact be grasped. This is because real communication and conversation depends, as the black theologians emphasize, on an awareness of difference. Without this awareness I am always in danger of constructing you in my own image, of assuming you mean what I mean, that your experience and perspective is identical with mine. It is only as we let others, other cultures and other periods of history, speak for themselves, that we can discern the distinctiveness that is the starting-point of true discourse. The very possibility of this discourse, as I have argued, assumes certain values in common. Indeed from a Christian point of view, we might go further than this to suggest that union and differentiation go together; that is, when there is real communication and communion between people, this brings out the distinctiveness and richness of the partners to the dialogue. Within the blessed Trinity a perfect unity goes with distinctiveness of persons and this is the pattern of true relationship.

We will, therefore, reject the eighteenth-century assumption that the values of European liberal intellectuals are universally

valid prior to and independently of any dialogue with other
cultures and other traditions. We will no less strongly reject the
view that an awareness of the difference between traditions must
automatically lead to a total relativism. An awareness of
difference is the starting-point, and on that basis it is possible to
discern widening areas of agreement. But this is, of its nature, an
unfinished task.

Chapter 10

THE PROTEST AGAINST GOD

The theme of this book is that the arguments put forward by Anthony Freeman do not stand up to examination. God is real and it is possible to know this. The assumptions of post-modernist deconstructionism are fallacious. Questions of meaning and truth remain on the agenda.

One of the weaknesses of using the word God to describe human values is the failure to respect atheism. Most people go through periods when the universe seems empty of God and life feels utterly bleak. Edwin Muir describes such a moment in his autobiography. Whilst he was working in a bone factory in Glasgow he travelled one day in a bus. Suddenly the passengers opposite him seemed nothing but animals, no longer made in the image of God, stripped of all spiritual grace. Muir was totally devastated and it took him a lifetime's spiritual pilgrimage to recover his earlier sense of the eternal in us. Some people never have or never recover this sense. Bravely, the best of such people develop a strong sense of pity for their fellow suffering, fellow struggling human beings. Such atheism deserves our proper respect. These are people who believe that life is devoid of any over-arching meaning, who think that existence, despite its shafts of beauty, is in the end tragic, and yet who simply choose to live for others rather than themselves. It is a noble stance.

Human companionship, affection and pity: all these are affirmed, defiantly asserted against the backdrop of a menacing world.

Yet Christians and those of other theistic faiths believe something different from this.

We believe that such human values go with the grain of the universe; that compassion echoes the heartbeat of a spiritual reality who is behind, beyond and within all things. Values are not a courageous bridge desperately thrown over a chasm of meaninglessness but a reflection of that God who moment by moment holds all things in being and who in the end will be 'all in all', as Paul put it.

There is a clear difference between atheism and theism. Atheists quite properly force us to choose between them. To dress up our human ideals and values and call them God simply fails to respond to the character of the world as we know it; it is grossly insensitive to the tragic dimension of human life, the suffering and evil which is always ready to engulf us. A Christian holds on to faith because of the cross of Christ; because of his resurrection and the hope that springs from it. But we know what atheism is and we can often be pulled into its orbit.

When George Eliot lost her faith in God she did not lose her sense of duty. On the contrary, the voice of duty spoke to her more insistently. But she was quite clear that this was a moral ideal and not a new name for the God in whom she had once believed. Respect atheism for what it is, a brave and often profoundly moral response to the world.

I have tried to indicate in this book that the case against the possibility of a wise and loving God behind this universe is a strong one, that needs to be taken with the utmost seriousness. In addition I believe that the protest against some traditional ways of talking about this God again need to be taken with due seriousness. More often than not these are protests that arise in the heart before the mind.

As I suggested in the first chapter, some traditional ways of speaking of God can seem oppressive, particularly today to women. The answer to this however is not to get rid of the idea of a transcendent God altogether but to explore the variety and richness of imagery which is present in biblical and Christian literature. To take just one example. In the Wisdom of Solomon, divine wisdom, which in Christian terms might be thought of either as the Holy Spirit, or the eternal Son of God, is described in these terms:

> For she is a breath of the power of God,
> And a pure emanation of the glory of the Almighty;
> Therefore nothing defiled gains entrance into her.
> For she is a reflection of eternal light,

A spotless mirror of the working of God,
And an image of his goodness.
Though she is but one, she can do all things,
And while remaining in herself, she renews all things;
In every generation she passes into holy souls
And makes them friends of God, and prophets;
For God loves nothing so much as the man
    who lives with wisdom.
For she is more beautiful than the sun,
And excels every constellation of the stars.
Compared with the light she is found to be superior,
For it is succeeded by the night,
But against wisdom evil does not prevail.
She reaches mightily from one end of the earth
    to the other,
And she orders all things well.
I loved her and sought her from my youth,
And I desired to take her for my bride,
And I became enamoured of her beauty.
              (Wisdom of Solomon, 7.25–82)

Then there is no doubt that some people find an excessively personalist way of talking about God difficult. I believe that personal language about God is essential and inescapable. For personal imagery can accommodate impersonal imagery but vice versa this is not true. If God is the highest we know then God cannot be less than personal. No modern theologian has been more convinced that we must address God as Thou', than Austin Farrer. But as a teenager he said he found this way of talking very difficult.

When Germans set their eyeballs and pronounced the terrific words, 'He speaks to Thee' I am sure, indeed, that they are saying something, but I am still more sure that they are not speaking to my condition.

In the modern world there are many people to whose condition such words are not saying anything. Farrer wrote that he found liberation from this impasse by thinking of God within himself.

I would no longer attempt, with the Psalmist, to set God
before my face. I would see him as the underlying cause of
my thinking, especially of those thoughts in which I tried to
think of him. I would dare to hope that sometimes my
thought would become diaphanous, so that there should be
some perception of the divine cause shining through the
created effect, as a deep pool, settling into a clear
tranquillity, permits us to see the spring at the bottom of it
from which its waters rise.[29]

This did not stop Farrer praying to God, or using personal
language when appropriate. But he no longer felt constricted or
oppressed by that language, as though it was the only legitimate
Christian way of thinking of praying. That is why I argued in an
earlier chapter that we can draw on the true God, who is truly in
us. God not only holds us in being and enfolds us with his love
but he fills us with his Spirit. We can seek to rest in and live
from his presence within us.

Freeman suggests that as we bring our human values and
ideals to bear in criticizing past pictures of God, so we ought
simply to assume that what we have are those human standards.
But those values and ideals are in the end rooted in God himself,
the source of all value. Nevertheless it is quite right that we
should use the judgement God has given us, including our sense
of moral discrimination to scrutinize all ideas and pictures,
however traditional. In religious terms, this means taking the
freedom which God has given us to engage in dialogue with God
himself. This is what Abraham did, when he pleaded with God
not to destroy a city. This is what Job did, when he refused to
accept pat answers about the cause of suffering. He wanted to
carry the argument to the face of God himself. The Jewish
tradition has on the whole been much bolder than the Christian
one in its willingness to argue with God, to have it out with him,
to bring moral standards to bear even to the extent of holding
God accountable to them. This may seem dangerous, even
presumptuous. But it is, I believe, the kind of freedom which
God gives us.

It is also true that some traditional religion has seemed too
other-worldly and disparaging of this life. For most people today
that is totally unacceptable. We want a Christian faith that

rejoices in the life that God has given us, that enjoys the world in which he has set us and the good things within it. But it is not necessary to kick God out of the way altogether in order to do this. On the contrary, this is a world about which he has said that it is very good, and it remains good however much we may despoil it.

The last time there was a major public debate about God was in the 1960s. Although the terms of that debate were rather different, I believe that the same motivating factors were present behind radical attempts to discard God. The debate reached its apogee when in 1966 *Time Magazine* printed a cover with the words 'God is dead' all over it. This was the thesis of the so-called 'God is dead' school of thought. Behind this, as behind other slightly less dramatic departures from traditional belief, was the feeling that we could only assert human responsibility if we got rid of God altogether; that we can only affirm this life if we discard the notion of another one; that we can only champion human autonomy if it is in no way constricted by the reality of a transcendent God. It was only if God, as it were, died, that we could live untrammelled lives, affirming this life.

The 'God is dead' school of thought passed as quickly as such fashions usually do. Only three years later *Time Magazine* published another cover indicating that God was alive again, and pointing its readers to the theology of hope and liberation theology, both of which orientate people towards the future. These two take human responsibility seriously, encouraging us to change the conditions in which human beings live, but they do so in a way which is congruous with traditional belief rather than a total departure from it.

I mention this past debate, not to go back into it, but to indicate that then, as now, there were serious issues about our whole understanding of God that needed to be addressed; but these can be addressed by theologies that are consonant with traditional belief. In short, in order to affirm this life, human responsibility and the duty of working for a better society, it is not necessary to think that the word God refers only to our human values and ideals. As we rejoice in the real God we rejoice in the good earth upon which we have been set; and we hear his call to eliminate justice and oppression, so that all may come to that fulfilment which he desires for his children. As we work to that end, we look forward to that consummation of his Kingdom when everything that is sick, cruel, destructive and ugly will be overcome and all will be well.

NOTES

1. Anthony Freeman, *God in Us: A Case for Christian Humanism*, SCM Press1993.

2. Simone Weil, *Waiting on God*, Collins 1959, p.120.

3. R.S. Thomas, 'Suddenly', *Later Poems*, Macmillan 1983, p.201.

4. T.S. Eliot, 'East Coker', *Four Quartets*, Faber and Faber 1944, 1.147.

5. W.H. Vanstone, *Love's Endeavour, Love's Expense*, DLT.

6. Janet Morley, *All Desires Known*, SPCK 1992, pp.9,27.

7. A full discussion of Providence, of how God relates to the world, lies outside the scope of this book. For a considered view see Keith Ward, *Divine Action*, Collins 1990.

8. James Joyce, *A Portrait of the Artist as a Young Man*, Penguin 1972, pp.169–71.

9. *A Portrait of the Artist as a Young Man*, p.253.

10. John Hick's, *Philosophy of Religion*, Prentice-Hall 1963, is a good introduction to the subject. In recent years the possibility of a natural theology has received increasing attention. For example, R. Swinburne, *The Existence of God*, Clarendon Press

1979, argues that there are intellectually compelling arguments for the reality of God.

11. Austin Farrer, *A Celebration of Faith*, ed. Leslie Houlden, Hodder and Stoughton 1970, p.61. Many of Austin Farrer's writings bear on the theme of this book. An anthology is available, edited by Richard Harries, *The One Genius*, SPCK 1987.

12. A.M. Allchin, The *Dynamic of Tradition*, DLT 1981, p.28.

13. Janet Martin Soskice 'Theological Realism' in *The Rationality of Religious Belief,* ed. William J. Abraham and Steven W. Holtzer, Clarendon Press 1987, p.118. The full argument is set out in Janet Martin Soskice, *Metaphor and Religious Language*, OUP 1985.

14. A sure-footed guide across the mudflats of post-modernism, especially as it bears upon the reading of biblical texts, is Anthony Thiselton, *New Horizons in Hermeneutics*, HarperCollins 1992.

15. Keith Thomas, *The Guardian*, 6 September, 1994.

16. E.P. Sanders, *The Historical Figure of Jesus,* Penguin 1993. This sceptical, cautious approach gives the minimum in the way of assured results. The minimum is worth having and its conclusions are as firm as any reconstruction of the past can be.

17. I have put the case for the resurrection of Christ in *Christ is Risen*, Mowbray 1987.

18. The report of the 1988 Lambeth Conference, *The Truth Shall Make You Free.* ACC 1988.

19. Julian of Norwich, *The Revelations of Divine Love*, Burns and Oates 1961, p.154.

20. *The Poems of Gerard Manley Hopkins*, ed. W.H. Gardner and N.H McKenzie, Oxford 1970, p.90.

21. H.A. Williams, *Poverty, Chastity and Obedience*, Mitchell Beazley 1975, p.24.

22. Richard Swinburne makes the point that in order for it to be my body that is recreated or reformed for eternity, there must be an identifiable self, i.e. a soul. My point is that we have no automatic entitlement to survive death. Our continuing identity depends upon God, his knowledge of us and his will for us to continue as the person we are.

23. Dietrich Bonhoeffer, *Letters and Papers from Prison*, The Enlarged Edition, SCM Press 1971, p.348.

24. Edwin Muir, 'One foot in Eden', *Collected Poems*, Faber and Faber 1960, p.227.

25. Rose Macaulay, *The Towers of Trebizond*, Collins 1956, p.288.

26. Evelyn Waugh, *Brideshead Revisited*, Penguin 1964, p.84.

27 Alasdair MacIntyre, *After Virtue*, Duckworth 1961, and 'A Partial Response to my critics' in *After MacIntyre* ed. John Horton and Susan Mendus, Polity Press 1994, pp.283ff

28. Katy Taylor, 'From Lavender to Purple',*Theology* September/October 1994.

29. Austin Farrer quoted in *The One Genius*, p.7.

PUBLICATIONS BY RICHARD HARRIES

BOOKS

Prayers of Hope, BBC 1975

Turning to Prayer, Mowbray 1978

Prayers of Grief and Glory, Lutterworth 1979

Being a Christian, Mowbray 1981; in the USA: *What Christians Believe*, Winston Press

Should a Christian Support Guerillas?, Lutterworth 1981

Praying Round the Clock, Mowbray 1983

The Authority of Divine Love, Blackwells 1983

Prayer and the Pursuit of Happiness, Collins 1985; in the USA: Eerdmans

Morning has Broken, Marshall Pickering 1985

Christianity and War in a Nuclear Age, Mowbray 1986

C.S. Lewis: The Man and his God, Collins 1987

Christ is Risen, Mowbray 1988

Is there a Gospel for the Rich? The Christian in a Capitalist World, Mowbray 1992

Art and the Beauty of God, Mowbray 1993

ANTHOLOGIES

Seasons of the Spirit (with George Every and Kallistos Ware), SPCK 1984; in the USA: *The Time of the Spirit*, St. Vladimir Seminary Press

The One Genius: Through the Year with Austin Farrer, SPCK 1987

EDITED AND CONTRIBUTED TO

What Hope in an Armed World?, Pickering and Inglis 1982

Reinhold Niebuhr and the Issues of our Time, Mowbray 1986; in the USA: Eerdmans

Stewards of the Mysteries of God (ed. E. James), Darton, Longman & Todd 1975

Unholy Warfare (ed. D. Martin and P. Mullen), Blackwell 1983

The Cross and the Bomb (ed. F. Bridger), Mowbray 1983

Dropping the Bomb (ed. J. Gladwin), Hodder & Stoughton 1985

Julian, Woman of our Time (ed. R. Llewellyn), Darton, Longman & Todd 1985
If Christ be not Raised (ed. J. Greenhalgh), St. Mary's, Bourne Street 1986

The Reality of God (ed. J. Butterworth), Severn House 1986

A Necessary End, Attitudes to Death (ed. J. Neuberger & J. White), Macmillan 1991 and SPCK 1987